# CONVERSATION FOR ACTION

# *Pragmatics & Beyond New Series*



10

Denise E. Murray

*Conversation for Action*

# CONVERSATION FOR ACTION

## THE COMPUTER TERMINAL AS MEDIUM OF COMMUNICATION

DENISE E. MURRAY
*San José State University*

JOHN BENJAMINS PUBLISHING COMPANY
AMSTERDAM/PHILADELPHIA

1991

**Library of Congress Cataloging-in-Publication Data**

Murray, Denise E.
Conversation for action : the computer terminal as medium of communication / Denise Murray.
p. cm. -- (Pragmatics & beyond, ISSN 0922-842X ; new ser. 10)
Includes bibliographical references and index.
1. Computer networks. 2. Interpersonal communication. I. Title. II. Series.
TK5105.5.M87 1991
306.4'4--dc20 91-27103
ISBN 90 272 5020 2 (Eur.)/1-55619-276-2 (US) (alk. paper) CIP

# Acknowledgments

This work reports on data collected at an IBM facility over an eight-month period. During this period, I observed the communication of a project manager, Les, and his colleagues. It is to Les and his colleagues that I owe my current understanding of communication patterns within their community. Without their cooperation and patient acceptance of my naive attempts to become part of the community, this study would not have been possible. To IBM I owe thanks for allowing me access to their equipment and working environment and especially to the two managers who wholeheartedly supported this venture: Jim Jordan, manager of the Los Angeles Scientific Center for arranging the study and for taking responsibility for my work; Paul Elerick, manager of the VLSI Systems Center, GTD Los Gatos, for giving me access to a mainframe computer to collect and analyze my data and ultimately to write up my results.

I would like to thank several other people for their contributions to this study: my husband, for his constant support, technical advice and encouragement throughout the writing of this book; John Godwin, IBM Research Division, San José, whose computer conversation with my husband first drew my attention to computer-mediated communication; Shirley Heath for recognizing the potential of such a study, for encouraging me to pursue and complete it, and for giving freely of her time during a very busy year; Terry Winograd, for his support and stimulating suggestions; Arthur Applebee for his encouragement; and Jef Verschueren and Bertie Kaal for their editorial help.

*For my parents—*
*Peter and Madge Stalley*
*for their encouragement of my education*

*and my husband, Bill*
*who introduced me to computer-mediated communication*

# Contents

# Settings and Actors

Throughout this study, the reader will be introduced to Les[1] and his colleagues from various IBM locations both within and outside the United States. These colleagues and locations (with network node[2]) are set out below for easy reference.

**IBM sites (with network node), employees and roles**

Park Lab, California (PARKVM)

| | |
|---|---|
| *Les Stretton* | Manager of Projects ROBIN, SEND and FALCON |
| *David Terry* | Director of Park Lab |
| *John McQueen* | Data Center Manager |
| *Simon Ashfield* | System Programmer |
| *Don Harrys* | Research Developer for Projects SEND and FALCON |
| *Brian Kelly* | Advisory Programmer |
| *Mary Wallace* | Project Developer |
| *Stuart Brandon* | Project Manager |

Mission Testing Lab, California (MSNVM)

| | |
|---|---|
| *Peter Munroe* | Data Center Manager |
| *Mat Weeks* | Tester for Project ROBIN |
| *Scott Davis* | System Programmer for Mission Lab |

El Monte Research Lab, California (ELMVM)

| | |
|---|---|
| *Ted Rogers* | System Programmer |
| *Jim Strong* | Liaison Manager for Project FALCON |
| *Guy Austin* | Programmer |

Pippin Research Lab, New York (PIPVM)

| | |
|---|---|
| *Sandy Priestly* | Technical Director of Project SEND |
| *Al Mason* | Personnel Director of Project SEND |
| *Robert Schmidt* | Liaison manager for Projects ROBIN and SEND |
| *Gordon Haydon* | Les's manager |

| | |
|---|---|
| *Herb Ryan* | Program Developer |
| *Susan Smirnoff* | Manager of Education Services |

Bermuda Lab, New York (BERVM)

| | |
|---|---|
| *Sid Taylor* | Liaison Manager for Project FALCON |

Companies Outside IBM

| | |
|---|---|
| NEWS | Company with equipment essential for Projects SEND and FALCON |
| BASC | Company leasing services to Projects SEND and FALCON |

# Transcription Conventions

Most of the data reported here comes from computer-mediated communication and is presented as it appeared on-line. Details of the conventions for mail and messages are given in Chapter 3. For easy reference, a brief overview is given below.

### Conventions used by computer-mediated communicators

| | |
|---|---|
| MSG FROM MSNVM(PETER) | indicates message arriving from NODE (MSNVM) and USERID (PETER) |
| msg msnvm(peter) | indicates message sent to NODE (msnvm) and USERID (peter) |
| ... | message/mail to continue OR new comment in same message/mail |
| .. | continuation of previous message/mail |
| *word* | emphasis |
| "word" or 'word' | name of system, program, node OR quotation |
| upper case in mixed case message/mail | name of system, program, node |
| u, ur, u r, r u | you, your, you are, are you |
| BTW, YW, CUL | by the way, you're welcome, catch you later |
| c /weds./tues/ | correction of error in previous message/mail |
| deletions | subject, copula, auxiliary, determiner |

| | |
|---|---|
| multiple vowels | rising intonation |
| ???? or !!!! | affect |

**Researcher's transcription conventions**

When lengthy conversations are reported and referred to in the text, speakers are identified by their first initial, followed by the number of the message. For example,

L1: Les's first message
B2: Brian's second message

For telephone or face-to-face conversations reported here, transcription conventions are

... missing data
(data) non-linguistic data

# Chapter 1

# INTRODUCTION

New technology both changes our lives and is itself changed as people apply it in their daily lives. We have witnessed the effects on our lives of telephones, television, and more recently, computers. However, when most people think of computers, they see them as word or number crunchers, machines that word process or execute complex problems. One vital but overlooked function computers can perform is communication, not person-machine communication, but communication between people, mediated via the computer.

It was the introduction of interactive computing and networks in the late 1960s that provided computer users with this new medium for communication: the computer terminal. Initially, computer-mediated communication (CmC) consisted of short one-liners used by technicians to solve immediate problems or to ask an operator to mount a tape. Today, CmC spans a range of activities from interactive messages to word processing. Electronic mail (E-mail) in particular has become pervasive: it is now used in homes, schools and any place where a computer can be linked to a telephone line or to another computer.

If, as Ong claims, "technology is important in the history of the word not merely exteriorly, as a kind of circulator of pre-existing materials, but interiorly, for it transforms what can be said and what is said" (1977:42), what has been the impact of this new medium on language and its use? How does an understanding of this new medium inform our understanding of language use in general? This study answers these questions with respect to CmC within a specific business community by exploring: (i) how computer communicators choose among the available media and modes of communication, and (ii) the basic and recurring discourse patterns across media and modes through which this community achieves its institutional goals of innovation and product development.

Despite the widespread use of CmC, little research has been conducted to examine the characteristics of discourse where the computer is the medium of communication (that is, messages sent and received electronically). To date, research of interest to linguists has concentrated on the effects of the computer in the work place for knowledge production and dissemination (e.g. Case 1984; Kling and Scacchi 1982), on the word processing function of the computer for creating extended prose, or on the human-machine interface, including developing models of language for machine recognition and production, in particular, artificial intelligence. Studies concerning the computer's word processing function have addressed the effect on the writing process when writers use a word processor (e.g. Bean 1983; Collier 1983; Daiute 1983; Bridwell et al. 1984; Bridwell et al. 1985; Vockell and Schwartz 1985; Van Pelt 1985); the effect on interest/motivation when writers use a word processor (e.g. Vockell and Schwartz 1985); the effect of text analysis programs on writing (e.g. Kiefer and Smith 1983); the adoption and use of computers by professors (Case 1984); and the composing process when dictating for transcription on a word-processor (Halpern and Liggett 1984). In such cases, however, the computer is not truly a medium of communication since the final product still appears in fixed print and only the means of production has changed.

Research on the human-machine interface has largely focussed on two areas. The first, a concern with human factors and the development of appropriate user interfaces, has examined the efficiency and "user-friendliness" of computer-user interfaces (e.g. Schneiderman 1980 on the use of menus and Card et al. 1983 on performance theory). The second area, a concern with developing machine recognition and production of language and information, is the field broadly defined as artificial intelligence (AI) and expert systems (see Dreyfus and Dreyfus 1986 for a recent discussion of AI). While this work does consider the computer as a medium of communication, it is communication between humans and machines, not human-human communication mediated via the computer.

Research that has examined the computer as a medium for human-human communication has identified a number of its characteristics: (i) computer conferencing leads to more democratic decision making but takes more time than face-to-face meetings (Hiltz and Turoff 1978); (ii) computer-mediated interaction is less inhibited than face-to-face interaction (e.g. Kiesler et al. 1984); (iii) because CmC is written, users develop written devices to indicate paralinguistic and non-linguistic cues (Carey 1980; Levodow 1980; and Murray 1985, 1988); (iv) time delay is the major cause of multiple threads in computer mail (Black et al. 1983); and (v) CmC facilitates student writing and participation (e.g. Quinn et al. 1983; Peyton and Batson 1986; Murray 1986). None of the research has examined how the introduction of the computer has affected choice[3] of medium and mode of communication or the structure of computer-mediated communication in relation to discourse purpose. This study shows how an examination of choice of different media and modes suggests the need to re-examine fundamental definitions of orality and literacy. Similarly, an examination of discourse structure in CmC provides a new way of thinking about discourse structure in general.

Data in this study show that the traditional dichotomous view and the more recent view of an oral/literate continuum are both oversimplifications of the phenomena and that medium (e.g. telephone, writing, face-to-face, computer terminal) and mode (e.g. meeting, casual conversation) do not themselves cause the appearance of certain characteristics. Rather, medium and mode are options whose choice depends on the context of situation (Halliday 1973). The choices appropriate to the context are socio-culturally defined, that is, "particular socially constructed technologies are used within particular institutional frameworks for specific social purposes" (Street 1984:97). If medium and mode are not independent for computer uses, what then contributes to the characteristics of writing compared with speaking (cf. Chafe 1982, Tannen 1982)?

This study suggests that medium and mode are not necessarily arbitrary but are options, the choice of a particular option being dependent on the context of situation. The particular characteristics of any particular speech event, including mode and medium, result from the context of situation. In other words, to explain the form and characteristics of any stretch of discourse, it is necessary first to determine the context in which the discourse is situated. Thus, I will establish principles for mode-switching, comparable to the notion of code-switching (Gumperz 1971). Further, conversation is not medium or mode dependent; conversations can be written, and one conversation may cross many media and modes, including a face-to-face episode, a telephone episode, a mail episode etc. Thus conversation is any interactive, cooperative linguistic exchange between two or more human beings (one may even wish to include internal conversations). Conversations can be created via exchange of letters, memos, audio tapes, video tapes etc. The basic recurring discourse pattern in the data discussed here is conversation for action, conversation that changes the status quo at one or both levels of language: ideational and interpersonal. This type of conversation contrasts with conversation to maintain social cohesion, which does not affect the status quo but confirms areas of solidarity and keeps participants' mutual knowledge up to date through confirmatory exchanges.

If we want to examine the effects of CmC on language use, it is necessary to situate CmC events within the broader sphere of language use. To do so affects both methodology and theoretical framework. Consequently, data in this study were collected through the traditional field methods[4] of the ethnographer: observation, participant-observation, formal and informal interviews, standard questionnaires, and collection of artifacts. Ethnographic methodology was chosen because it provides for ecologically valid participant observation which in turn provides data spanning all language use by those observed. Between September 1984 and June 1985, I spent from 20 to 30 hours a week collecting data as an observer in an IBM research laboratory. Since then I have spent summers at the same site, continuing this research. I focussed observations on a technical project manager (Les Stretton[5]) in his office, in meetings, in the hallways, at lunch, on the telephone and on-line. Over the eight months as an observer, I participated in the life of this field setting by acquiring CmC skills, increasingly incorporating electronic mail and other uses of the computer into my own repertoire of language use.

In the chapters that follow, we will trace the communicative strategies of Les and his colleagues over a period of eight months. We will listen in to their meetings, face-to-face conversations and read their electronic mail and messages. We will see how they interact in offices, in hallways, in meeting rooms and on-line. We will follow Les from Park Lab in California to Pippin Lab in New York. We will meet colleagues working with Les on his projects, colleagues requesting his expert help on technical matters, visitors from outside companies, and colleagues he meets by chance as he goes about his daily work. We will see how they make use of the communicative resources available to them; how the communicative choices they make affect their communication; how the choices themselves index communication; and the way communication is structured by individual and institutional goals.

Part I asks "Who speaks what language to whom and when?" (Fishman 1965) within this particular community of computer users. Part II discusses approaches to studying language in context from several different disciplines, showing that current theories of language use do not account for the nature of the communicative work in which Les and his colleagues engage. I then suggest a framework for examining when speakers switch or use particular modes. Chapter 7 then develops this framework into a taxonomy of aspects of context of situation which influence medium/mode choice. Part III shows how current theories of conversational structure do not account for these data. I then develop a model for the structure of the recurring conversations engaged in by Les and his colleagues: conversation for action and in particular, collaborative information development. Part IV discusses how this model of conversation can be applied to other institutional settings and how it provides a framework for understanding language in use.

# PART I:

# THE WEB OF COMMUNICATION

The metaphor of a "web" has been used by various scholars. Culture is the webs man has spun and in which he is suspended (Geertz 1973); computerization is the web of social processes for organizing social life with computers (Kling and Scacchi 1982); leadership is a web of symbolic action and language (Tierney 1985); language is the web in which James Murray constructed his dictionary world (Murray 1979); and writing is the structuring of the web of meaning (Vygotsky 1962). I use web here to highlight the complex interaction among language, communication tools and social context. The community both spins this web and is caught in it. To understand the complexity of the web, the researcher approaches it both from outside and from the point of view of the community itself.

Part I provides the contextual frame in which communication takes place. In Chapter 2, we will meet Les in his work environment to get a general perspective of "a day in the life of . . .". We will thereby have a picture of who speaks what language to whom and when. Chapter 3 identifies the language resources available to Les and his colleagues at their most general level, that is, who speaks *what language* to whom and when. Chapter 4 describes the networks of interaction Les engages in with his colleagues, that is, who speaks what language *to whom* and when. Chapter 5 identifies the contexts in which Les and his colleagues use the different media available to them, that is, who speaks what language to whom and *when*.

# Chapter 2

# WORKING AT PARK LAB

**Tuesday, October 1984**

*10:00 a.m.* Les Stretton sits at his desk facing two computer terminals. On one, he has just received a message from Joe in Sweden requesting information. On the other, he is browsing through his files trying to find the one containing the information he knows is there and he needs at the moment. Behind to his right on the opposite wall is an IBM PC. He finds the information he's looking for, sends off several messages to Joe and Joe responds with other questions that Les also answers. The phone rings. It's the secretary of another department, trying to set up a meeting. She asks if next Monday is OK, Les says he'll be out of town Monday through Wednesday and suggests Thursday or Friday. They agree on Friday and she says she'll call back once she's checked with everyone invited to the meeting. Meanwhile, Joe asks other questions and Les responds. Al walks in and asks where the floppy disks for the PC are. Les tells him, pointing to the shelf over his PC. Al goes over, searches through the manuals, finds the one he wants, and goes out, saying "I've got the Pascal compiler. I'll bring it back later". Meanwhile, on his first terminal, Les has exited from the file with the information Joe wanted and returned to the technical work he was doing before Joe's message came.

*11:20.* Les checks his E-mail. He finds five pieces of mail. He immediately answers four using E-mail. He doesn't know the answer to the question in the fifth one. He uses the other terminal to browse through his files but can't locate the one with the necessary information. He leaves the mail for later and goes back to the program he was writing.

*14:30.* Les has both terminals and the PC running. He's on the phone to Mat, who's testing code Les has been writing. There are still bugs in the code and, while running it, it's got hung.[6] Mat wants Les to tell him how to free it. Then two messages flash across Les's screen:

FROM PARKVM(SIMON): yo. you there?
FROM PARKVM(SIMON): ok, we's all heading out de door to 999 now

Les has a meeting with the support group at Park Lab and Peter, the data center manager from Mission Testing Lab, to discuss plans for cooperation on testing software for one of Les's projects (Project SEND). After the internal meeting, representatives from an outside company (NEWS) are coming to discuss their hardware, which Les hopes to use for the project. He got caught up on the phone to Mat. Simon tried to call to remind him of the meeting, but the line was busy, so he sent the humorous message above to let Les know the meeting is about to start. Les logs off both terminals and the PC, leaves his office, and heads for the meeting room.

**Meeting room 999**

John, the manager of the data center at Park Lab, and Peter discuss how they can link their centers together to test the new technology. Les gives them the technical details on the hardware and the current status of the software. They determine the questions they will ask the representatives from NEWS, the outside company.

*15:50.* Les returns to his office. Outside the meeting room, Peter, Research Developer Don, and John and his system programmer, Simon, discuss how they can cooperate and write code to support the hardware. This represents a new direction of interest for Simon and Don who had previously thought this particular code unnecessary.

*16:30.* Peter leaves the group and goes down to Les's office. They discuss how they can work together to develop another project involving Scott (Peter's system programmer). Les will work with Scott on the software, and Peter will encourage him to participate. They then move on and discuss implementing new code on Peter's system.

*17:30.* Les's phone rings. Mat has another problem. Peter says "Thanks, Les" and leaves the office. Les solves Mat's problem before returning to his own work.

**Wednesday**

Les checks his E-mail and finds a note from Peter setting out his summary of the decisions reached at Tuesday's meeting. The mail includes Peter's commitment to buy some more equipment from NEWS.

**Friday, May 1985**

*6:30 p.m.* Les, Peter and several others involved in project SEND are having dinner at a local cafe. Les tells Peter that NEWS has introduced its new equipment and will upgrade any current equipment, the upgrades costing far less than buying new units. Peter is excited because he had planned to buy several more pieces of NEWS old equipment. Now, he can upgrade what he already has, buy some new pieces, and thereby have a more powerful service without additional expense.

Park Lab is a small research laboratory in the foothills of Silicon Valley. Les Stretton has worked for IBM for over 20 years, writing operating systems and now also directing several new projects. Les has an individual office with two computer terminals and an IBM PC, which can be linked to the mainframe computer. His office[7] is at the end of a dead end corridor, so he has little contact with people just passing by. He has access to six different computer systems and has two USERIDs on each. A USERID is the name chosen by a computer user for identification by the system and by other users and, within IBM, is limited to eight characters. People make many different choices of USERID: given name, family name, initials, and cute names. Les's two USERIDs are LES and STRETTON. Les uses the different USERIDs to partition his files according to projects. He uses his ID on ELMVM for communication (in addition to technical work). Most people send mail and messages to him at that USERID and NODE. Consequently, one of his terminals is usually logged on to ELMVM(STRETTON). If he receives a message at another ID and NODE he may ask the sender to 'please send to STRETTON at ELMVM' if he does not want his other work interrupted.

Each computer system has its own identification name or NODE, which is usually an abbreviation of the actual name of the IBM location. Many NODE names include VM for virtual machine, referring to the operating system used at these locations. Through IBM's world-wide interactive network connecting more than 1500 mainframe computers, employees are able to communicate almost instantaneously with any other employee on the network.

Les, like many employees, has a terminal (or IBM PC) at home which he uses to connect (log on) to the mainframe computer at Park Lab. By using a special program and telephone lines, he can also log on to one of his own NODEs from another NODE. Thus, Les may be on the East Coast but can be logged on to one of the six systems he has access to on the West Coast. Indeed, he may be using the computer to chat with someone in the same physical building on the East Coast, but the messages are routed via the West Coast. If he had a USERID for the computer system in the building he would, of course, be able to connect directly.

Over the past several years, Les has been managing three major projects. One project (Project ROBIN), which is now completed, involved writing code for a new product and testing the code in another location (Mission Testing Lab) a few miles away. At the time of this study, the code was written, had been tested, and, apart from minor modifications, was ready for inclusion in the company's product. Since the conclusion of this study, it has become an integral part of an IBM product. The other two projects (SEND and FALCON) are more complex, involving new hardware and software development, and are still in their infancy. Both involve people across the country and people outside IBM. Consequently, Les is constantly travelling around the country to negotiate and advise on the status of both projects. Project SEND involves a team led by Al Mason and Sandy Priestly located at Pippin Lab in New York. Al and Sandy frequently come out to Park Lab to consult with colleagues on the West Coast. During these visits, they use an office in the same corridor as Les at Park Lab.

In addition to these formal projects, Les is responsible for several software products and is often called on for his expertise in several areas. He was previously a system programmer at El Monte Research Lab and has remained close to many El Monte colleagues who often seek his advice and thus form one major group of his interactants.

Les has the support of several colleagues at Park Lab, in particular John, a long-time IBM employee who manages the data center for the lab. He is responsible for keeping the computers running and satisfying the computing needs of the project groups that use the lab computers. Reporting to him are Simon, who is a system programmer, and Don Harrys, a software developer who is writing code for projects SEND and FALCON. Both Simon and Don are essential to Les's work. Brian works on a very different project, but both his and Les's work are interdependent. In addition to their interdependence in work, Les, John, Simon, Don and Brian are old friends, often have lunch together and frequently meet socially.

To get his project work done, Les collaborates closely with colleagues at the El Monte Research Laboratory and the Mission Testing Laboratory, both of which are several miles away. Jim from the El Monte Research Lab and Peter from the Mission Testing Lab provide facilities for testing SEND and FALCON, with links to the Bermuda Lab on the East Coast (in cooperation with Sid).

While much of Les's work is technical, in his capacity as project manager he is responsible for planning, organizing and implementing hardware and software and hiring and directing project personnel. As a result, more and more of his time is being spent on communication: from casual face-to-face interaction over lunch to formal documents and presentations.

# Chapter 3

# WHO SPEAKS WHAT LANGUAGE

What language resources are available to Les and his colleagues? I will answer this question at the broadest level of media and then for the modes considered salient by the IBM VM[8] community and to an outside observer—in this case, myself as participant observer. Within the work environment, Les can choose from among a variety of communication media, some of which have characteristics peculiar to the organization and technology within IBM in general and at Park Lab in particular.

Terms such as channel, medium, and mode are used differently in different disciplines and even variously within the same discipline and therefore require explanation. Hymes (1972), for example, says that *channel* refers to the *medium* of transmission of speech, such as oral or written, thus conflating two potentially useful terms. Halliday (1973), on the other hand, uses *mode* to refer both to *medium*, which is Hymes' channel, and to the relation between language and what it is talking about. Other scholars use the terms loosely and often interchangeably. Duranti (1986), in discussing Hymes' category of channel goes on to talk of *medium* for communication such as writing and *modes* of oral communication as *forms* or *styles*.

Given the inconsistency in use of these terms by other scholars, I will define how I will use channel, medium, and mode in this study. Channel refers to the pre-theoretical sensory modalities. For communication through language, three of the available channels are used: visual, aural and tactile. Writing, for example, makes use of visual and tactile channels, while braille makes use of tactile, and telephone conversations utilize the aural channel. Medium refers to established methods of communication through language, each of which uniquely bundles channels. Les and his colleagues use face-to-face, telephone, computer terminal, and print media for communication. Mode refers to specific communication types within a medium, such types being socio-culturally defined. As previously mentioned, within linguistics and other disciplines, mode, genre, and style are often used interchangeably. I will use mode since genre is often associated solely with literary types such as narrative and style with a way of speaking or writing at the level of syntax and semantics (and possibly phonology) and thus describes language use closer to register. As used here, mode includes socio-culturally defined forms and functions. A more complete discussion of genre is given in Chapter 6.

Thus, for print media, newspapers and books are classified as two different modes, and for face-to-face media, meetings and casual conversation would be two different modes.

What media and modes are used by Les and his colleagues? Media include face-to-face, telephone, computer terminal, and print, which are discussed below. The various modes used are also discussed under each medium.

### 1. Face-to-face communication

Face-to-face communication occurs one-to-one and in groups; it occurs in formal meetings and presentations and informal chance meetings over lunch or in the corridors. John comes down to Les's office to ask him a question or stops him in the corridor. Les calls a meeting for all those involved in a project. During the meeting, information is exchanged, and responsibilities and work assignments are negotiated. After the meeting, people fall into small groups outside the meeting room and in Simon's office. The discussions continue and more negotiations are made.

On one of his trips East, Les makes a formal presentation on the general principles of FALCON to a group of interested software developers. After the presentation, several colleagues speak to him informally and others arrange for Les to see them in their offices for more detailed conversations. The next day, Les visits the Pippin Research Laboratory to talk with the group working on SEND. Les arranges to meet Sandy and Al (the two directly managing the project for Les) in the cafeteria to talk about the current status of the project, but arrives before them. As he walks into the cafeteria, he sees a group of colleagues he knows sitting talking around a table. They ask him to join them. They are, in fact, meeting to discuss the current status of their own project. Les quickly becomes part of the discussion, and the others ask his advice and draw on his expertise. He has information concerning forthcoming hardware they intend to use. They quickly learn that they will have to adapt their work to this new hardware. The meeting breaks up, with the project group eager to make use of the new technology. Les moves over to join Sandy and Al who came into the cafeteria while he was talking with the other group.

Thus negotiations are made and information exchanged as a result of both formally called meetings and chance encounters. In these face-to-face encounters, the three available channels are used in the chosen mode of communication.

## 2. Telephone

Les receives many telephone calls but rarely initiates a call, unless it is to someone outside the company who is not tied into the IBM computer network. By preference, he chooses CmC. If he is out of his office, the message center at Park Lab types the message onto the terminal, and sends it to Les who receives it when he next checks his mail on-line. When there is a message to call someone, he does it immediately. However, he is constantly frustrated because the person is not in his/her office, and he has to leave a message. A trail of messages often results with the two principals never making contact, a phenomenon referred to in the company as *telephone tag*.

While on the telephone, Les continues to work at the computer terminal. Sometimes the call is technical, and he brings up the program or information file and relays the information to the caller. In one such case Mat calls Les on the telephone and tells him of a problem he had while running the program he is testing for Les. He also sends him an on-line copy of the trace made of the execution of the program. During this conversation, Les works on two terminals. On one he calls up the code for the program, and on the other he has the trace of the problem. In the excerpt below, Les changes the program and orally recounts these changes to Mat. Telephone conversations were not audio recorded for legal reasons and so we have only some of Les's side of the conversation from my observations. Mat speaks between each of Les's contributions. "..." indicates data not manually recorded.

(1) *Les*: let's just remove that one piece and see what happens
*Les*: if we do that ... if specify cylinder ... you IPL 190 without parameter, cylinder gets set to zero ... basically reads record one
*Les*: if you want to have ... nucleuses on ... cylinder 98 and 99 reserved for IPL ... alternate ... if something went wrong could always drop back to prior nucleus ...
*Les*: if you just IPL 190 that shouldn't have any effect on it
*Les*: let's see if I can ... I go into here, say IPL 190 ...
*Les*: ok, which one didn't work? ok ok
*Les*: so show ... do I get to the
*Les*: I've got that set up OK now I IPL 190 ...
*Les reads from the screen.*
*Les*: he wants to read into record zero, ok

*(looks at program on second terminal—bangs desk lightly—scans through program—goes to fulist[9] and sends file to Mat)*

*Les*: that should fix that problem. I've removed for right now the capability of specifying the cylinder number . . . before it said replace didn't . . . I replaced with . . . so if you specify cylinder number it isn't going to work . . . I'm going to have . . .

*Les*: as long as you don't specify cylinder number it should work ok

During this telephone conversation, while running the program and trying to find the bug, Les uses two different ways of referring to the program: he identifies with the program, calling it I, and he refers to the program as he. Both uses are very common in oral conversation among programmers who describe programs dynamically as if a person were in the program carrying out the instructions. Such personalization of the program is not, however, considered appropriate in formal writing such as program documentation or professional articles in journals.

## 3. Computer-mediated communication

CmC refers here to any human-human communication mediated via a computer. CmC includes the following modes, listed in order from the mode with the most potential for immediate interaction to the mode with the least.

1. Computer Messages
2. Computer Mail
3. Computer Conferencing
4. Forums
5. Bulletin Boards
6. Documents
7. Bill Boards (e.g. HELP files)

### 3.1 *Computer Messages*

Computer Message (E-message) refers to the interchange of one-line messages between two or more participants simultaneously logged on to computer terminals. The message length when typing and when received is controlled by the system and is system specific. Thus, the details described here are peculiar to the IBM VM system observed in this study. In this system, sender text is restricted to two lines of text. Once senders type these lines, they must either send the message by hitting the enter key or abort the message. In this particular IBM system, text is not entered into the computer until the user hits the enter (execution) key. The system then breaks the message up into blocks, the number of characters per block depending on several different programs in the network code and also depending on programs at each node (but is at least 80 characters). Some nodes truncate the message and the extra characters are lost. Therefore, many users limit their input text to one line or 80 characters so that the system does not break the message in the middle of a word. Often people want to send more than 80 characters and so send consecutive messages. They usually indicate they have more to send by typing ... at the end of each message. However, they must retype the recipient's USERID (and NODE if the recipient is on a different system) for each message. To facilitate sending multiple messages, many users assign a retrieve function to one of their PF keys.[10] When they press this key, the previous command they typed returns to the screen, but is not executed and may be modified. Previous commands are stacked so they can return to whichever command they want. These commands are often used during interactive messaging to save having to retype USERID and NODE for each message; instead, the user presses the retrieve PF key and types over the previous message. This action can lead to unplanned results. If the user is conversing with more than one person, s/he may overtype a previous message to a different person from the one intended or may inadvertently leave part of a previous message in the new one. This function is also used to repeat the same message if it gets lost or the recipient doesn't respond. For frequent correspondents, Les keeps a nickname file so that he only has to type the message command and the nickname of the recipient. For example, if Les is logged on at El Monte Research Lab and Brian is logged on at Park Lab, to send a message to Brian, Les types

(2a) v brian problem went away with command in front of forward/back

However, if Brian's USERID and NODE were not in his nickname file, he would have to type

(2b) vmsg parkvm(briank) problem went away with command in front of forward/back

If they had both been logged on to the same computer system, the NODE would have been unnecessary. Thus, Les would have typed only the command and Brian's USERID as follows:

(2c) msg briank problem went away with command in front of forward/back

Each E-message is received separately and the system converts all sent E-messages to upper case unless the sender has installed a special mixed case program. Les does not use a mixed case program and so he used only lower case in the E-message above to Brian, knowing that the system automatically converts it to upper case. Brian received this E-message in the following form

(2d) FROM ELMVM(LES): PROBLEM WENT AWAY WITH COMMAND IN FRONT OF FORWARD/BACK

ELMVM is the NODE for the El Monte Research Laboratory where Les is logged on, and LES is his USERID.

As we can see in this example, the system automatically inserts the USERID of the sender before the E-message. If the E-message comes from a different NODE, the system automatically inserts both the USERID and the NODE of the sender, as in the above example. Had they both been logged on to the same system, Brian would have received the E-message in the following form:

(2e) MSG FROM LES: PROBLEM WENT AWAY WITH COMMAND IN FRONT OF FORWARD/BACK

This difference in commands and form for E-messages depends only on where the sender and recipient are logged on; not on where they are physically. Thus, Les could be physically at Park Lab, but be logged on to the El Monte Research Lab system and so would have to indicate NODE when sending an E-message to Brian who is logged on to the Park Lab system. Similarly, when Les is on the East Coast, recipients (even on the East Coast) receive E-messages prefixed by the El Monte NODE and Les's USERID: ELMVM(LES).

Conversations through E-messages are asynchronous because of the time delay in typing an E-message and in sending it electronically. Touch typists such as Les are able to generate more discourse faster than one-finger typists and Les is sometimes accused of over-riding his conversational partner. However, even for touch typists, it still takes longer to type an E-message than to say the same thing orally. Further, the electronic delay is uncertain. Depending on network traffic and the state of software and hardware, an E-message from New York to California or from one office to another down the hall can take less than a second or can take minutes or even longer. Thus, in a typical interaction, there is overlap: one partner may be still in the middle of typing an E-message when another E-message arrives and invalidates the E-message in progress. The sender may therefore abort or change the E-message in progress. If interactants want to coordinate their conversations, they have to wait for one E-message to arrive before sending their own. Because such waiting is not time efficient, most regular users overlap and interweave E-messages as we can see in the following example:

(3) msg ted what is xedit/macro command to extract line from file . . . in lower case
MSG FROM TED: . . TO PUT INTO ANOTHER FILE?

msg ted    instead of 'stack'
msg ted    which gets line in upper case
MSG FROM TED: . . GEE, I DON'T KNOW
msg ted    i want the line into rex in mixed case

Ted's question arrives on Les's screen before he has finished all he wants to say. Les continues with his turn, however, ignoring Ted's question. In other cases, the answer comes before the sender has time to complete the turn and so the sender does not send it.

Because of the time delay in typing the E-message, computer communicators claim they have developed informal conventions to reduce the number of keystrokes. Because E-messages are written, there are no paralinguistic and non-linguistic cues. As a result, computer communicators are developing written realizations of such cues. Examples of such conventions include syntactic simplification, abbreviations, and semi-conventionalized markers as detailed below.

1. *Syntactic simplification*
   - subject deletion
   - auxiliary deletion
   - determiner deletion

   The following example has subject (we), auxiliary (will) and determiner (a) deleted:

(4a) (we) (will) have to set up (a) special procedure

   - copula deletion

(4b) (are) you going to take several weeks vacation while you are here?

   - subject and copula/auxiliary deletion

(4c) (I am) currently in park . . . (I will) be by later

2. *Abbreviations*
   - u, ur, u r, r u for you, your, you are, and are you.
   - BTW, YW, CUL for by the way, you're welcome, catch you later
   - thot, enuf, gime for thought, enough, give me
   - c /weds./tues/ to tell the recipient there was an error or typo in a previous message.

3. *Markers*
   - *text*: asterisks are used to indicate emphasis

(4d) please call—we've *got* to discuss

– Multiple vowels are used for rising intonation (e.g. "sooooo")
– Multiple ? or ! are used to indicate affect

(4e) well how did things go yesterday???

– ... to indicate that the message is to continue but will not fit into one message
– you there / hi as a summons. (See Chapter 9 under conversational openings for detailed explanation.)

4. *Quotation marks/Case*
   – 'text'/TEXT: single quotation marks or upper case are used to indicate either a computer system/node/command/name or a repeat of something either partner has already said. See below for an explanation of this convention.

Many conventions follow computer commands, for example, "c/.../..." is the editing command to change text. When editing, the command "c /weds./tues/" would change "weds." to "tues" in the actual text. Other conventions have developed from the names of programs, for example, gime is a command that invokes a program that links the user to another disk. Still other strategies come from general use, such as tonite. Although these strategies first developed in E-messages in order to reduce key strokes and therefore typing time, many have since found their way into E-mail as well. The following E-message conversation dramatically illustrates the use of simplification strategies.

(4f) P1: I HOPE WE CAN FIND AN OPPORTUNITY TO TALK PRIVATELY TONITE – OR SOMETIME
P2: SOON IF NOT TONITE
P3: WHEN U GOING TO CAFE?
L1: 35 minutes, you want to come over before & talk?
P4: NO – MAYBE WE CAN FIND AN OPPORTUNITY TONITE

Until recently, the computer system converted all sent E-messages to upper case. Thus, senders typed only in lower case. Because upper case could not be used as a marker, various conventions developed. One is the use of *...* for emphasis as shown above. Another is the use of quotation marks to indicate either the name of a system, program or a quotation of what another person had said. Recently, however, programs are being used that allow both upper and lower case, and these are becoming more popular. In at least one location (Pippin Lab), a mixed case program is the default. Users there say mixed case is "more elegant" or "more sophisticated". However, this is a period of transition and confusion can arise, as the following example demonstrates:

(5) S1: you might be interested in the results of USERS (STILL to show

you a bit about performance
M1: yes – what should i do to get the info?
S2: say "USERS (STILL". If you want more explanation, try "USERS ?"
M2: i *did* say users (still and i got back no!
S3: oh, well, then read the help text USERS ? and consider ipling to get the latest shared system

In this example, Simon used mixed case and Mary did correctly interpret upper case as the system command she should use. She tried it, but it did not work, so she assumed she had made an error. Rather than explain all this to Simon, she sent a short E-message (M1). Simon, however, assumed she had misinterpreted the upper case and so reverted to the established convention of using quotation marks.

E-messages are not filed and last for the life of the screen only. Once the screen scrolls forward, there is no record of the E-message on the screen or in a file. The screen may scroll before the recipient has read the E-message because s/he had previously executed some command that was filling the screen. There is no efficient way of retrieving lost E-messages. Conversationalists do not have a hard copy to circle back to when memory for what they and their partners have written needs jogging, as in pen-in-hand, computer writing, or even E-mail. When an E-message arrives during technical work, the work already in progress can force the screen to advance and the recipient loses the E-message. The following is an amusing example where Simon repeats his E-message to Les (using his retrieve PF key) multiple times and finally types "zzzzzz" to indicate he's fallen asleep waiting for a reply.

(6) MSG FROM SIMON: has Campbell sent you SOOP MODULE?
msg simon please repeat, screen cleared
MSG FROM SIMON: has Campbell sent you SOOP MODULE?
MSG FROM SIMON: has Campbell sent you SOOP MODULE?
MSG FROM SIMON: has Campbell sent you SOOP MODULE?
MSG FROM SIMON: has Campbell sent you SOOP MODULE?
MSG FROM SIMON: zzzzzz
msg simon sorry, was in the middle of some screens, no he hasn't

This strategy is typically employed when the lost E-message is the initiation of an interaction or provides important content. However, it is not time efficient to constantly ask for repetition of forgotten discourse. Thus, interactants have to rely on memory to track the conversation or, if they want to be sure they will cover everything in the original request, they will move to E-mail. Another aspect of channel in E-messaging is the dynamic but ambiguous use of silence. Because the oral/aural channels are not available, silence cannot be interpreted as refusal or negative. Indeed, most computer communicators assume silence as a positive response.

In the following example, Les does not receive a reply to his question for 13 minutes; yet he accepts this silence as normal.

(7) 15:33:47 *Les*: well how did things go yesterday????
15:34:17 *Les*: . . 3.3?
15:47:50 *Mat*: Very well. No 3088 problems at all

Naive users, however, take time to adjust to this convention as the following example illustrates:

(8) 15:34:50 M1: am getting and reading files ok. to load on disk, do i . . .
M1: 'disk load' or 'receive' – which better?
15:42:51 L1: have to set up special procedure

The time gap between Mary's question and Les's response is shorter than in Example 7 above. Yet because Mary was then a naive user, when she receives no immediate response, she checks to see if Les is logged on. He is. She then checks if he has sent mail by looking in her reader. No mail. She again checks if he is logged on. Finally, his reply (L1) comes.

Recently, there has been widespread discussion of ways to avoid ambiguity and misinterpretation resulting from the absence of oral/aural channels. Suggestions (largely tongue-in-cheek) have included the use of computer drawn icons representing smiling faces etc. These icons are typed using regular characters, but inline icons have to be read sideways. Suggestions include:

(:-( to represent a frowning face

):-) to represent a smiling face

:<) for those with hairy lips

:<)= for those with beards

```
+  -
  |    Used for subtle humor
\_/

\ /
  |    Used for biting humor
\_/

o o
  |    Used for tongue-in-cheek humor
((_ /
```

While ambiguities and misinterpretations do occur, CmC within this community fulfills interpersonal functions and is considered appropriate unless real damage is likely to occur to interpersonal relations. Within the IBM VM community, the system of E-messages functions because users know its special rules.

If the recipient is logged on, the E-message appears on the screen, interrupting the terminal session when s/he next hits the enter key. Many people find E-messages disruptive because they have to interrupt the work they are currently doing. They can, however, choose not to receive E-messages. This is done primarily because E-messages also include information messages from the system. When a user sends mail or a file to someone in the network, s/he is informed of every step in the network that the file passes through. These messages can fill the screen constantly and prevent the user from doing any other work. Therefore, many users choose to turn messages off. In the current system, this also means they cannot receive E-messages, as well as system messages. When a sender sends an E-message to a user who has made this choice, s/he receives the message "NOT RECEIVING". Thus, the sender has to choose another medium or mail.

At Pippin Lab (the location which has mixed case as the default), several people use the "NOT RECEIVING" command to filter messages. They write a program that assumes that all E-messages from people are in mixed case and all system messages are in upper case. The program then displays only mixed case messages on the screen and discards upper case messages. However, the program then discards E-messages from potential communicators who do not use a mixed case program. Consequently, users of non-mixed case have to use E-mail to communicate with Pippin Lab colleagues. These colleagues at Pippin Lab feel mixed case is "more elegant" and "human", prefer to have dialogues in mixed case and so are willing to forego E-message dialogues with non-mixed case users.

If the recipient is not logged on, the sender receives a system message "X NOT LOGGED ON" and the E-message is lost. There is a third state in which users can disconnect their terminals from the system, but leave their USERID active. The active USERID may be left in an idle state in which case the sender receives the system message "X DISCONNECTED" and the E-message is lost. However, a disconnected USERID may be left with a program running. Internal programs are available that allow users to respond automatically when disconnected and that store the incoming E-messages. One such program is called GONE. When users disconnect, they call up the GONE program and type in a reply message, for example:

(9) GONE TO FALCON MEETING 13:30 ROOM 999. BACK 15:00.

When colleagues send an E-message or a file, the system automatically responds with this message and an indication that the file or E-message has been received.

During this study, Les began using a special program that collects and stores all incoming E-messages and system messages without disrupting terminal use. Les frequently accesses this store by requesting that all stored E-messages be displayed on the screen. He can then quickly scan the terminal for conversation E-messages and reply to them. This program is not a company product and is not bug free. However, it does facilitate receipt of E-messages.

### 3.2 *Computer Mail*

Computer Mail (E-mail) refers to extended text that is sent and received via the computer. If recipients are not logged on, the E-mail is stored in their file (reader) and they can access it when they next log on. If they are logged on, the computer displays a brief message on the screen, indicating the delivery of the mail. The recipient then has to access the reader file to read the E-mail. The recipient may respond immediately or later. Several different E-mail facilities are available within the company and many people adapt their local E-mail tool to meet their own particular needs. In general, users have a prologue and/or epilogue to their E-mail, in which any or all of the following may be inserted: sender's USERID, NODE, ADDRESS, TELEPHONE NUMBER; recipient's USERID and NODE; the SUBJECT and the DATE. For example:

(10) Date: 29 May 1985, 09:38:28 PDT
From: Mary A. Wallace Tie-line 999-9999 MARY at PARKVM
To: MASON at PIPVM
Subject: questionnaire
Yes, I did get your completed questionnaire. Thank you very much.
Regards,
M.

Les has a program that automatically reads all the files in his reader that look like E-mail files and then puts them into one long file on his disk. When he wants to check his E-mail, he uses another program he has written that places him at the point where he last finished reading in the E-mail file. He checks his E-mail frequently and responds to most E-mail immediately. Sometimes, he does not have the information to hand and so leaves responding until later. Hence he can forget that he has not responded because the E-mail is all in one concatenated file and he has no way of knowing whether he has responded or not. Other people file their E-mail in separate files for each correspondent.

This causes a problem in cross-referencing when more than one person receives E-mail and/or one topic concerns more than one person. Managers in particular say they would like a filing system that allows E-mail to be read according to sender/recipient and according to topic. Further, they would like to be able to track outstanding promises they have made, promises made to them, requests they've made that have not been met and requests made of them that they have not fulfilled. In fact, managing the enormous quantity of E-mail is one of the problems of the modern office. The amount of E-mail has proliferated because it is simple to send unfocused E-mail via the computer. This unfocused E-mail may be in one of the following forms:

- ... fyi. This may be appended to a piece of E-mail sent by a third party. If there is no further communication, how should the receiver respond? Is it really a request to act on the information or is it only background information? While fyi is done with hard copy printed materials, it is done more frequently with E-mail and is unsolicited. With hard copy, it usually follows a discussion on the existence of the material, followed by the suggestion that it may be of interest to the other person.
- cc. It is indeed simple to send the same piece of E-mail to a large number of people. There is evidence that people use large distribution lists and fail to update them or check that the material would really be relevant to all the recipients. Data from this study show many instances when people request that they be taken off distribution lists in order to cut down on the amount of incoming E-mail
- junk mail. It is equally simple to forward a file to another or many recipients. In my time as participant observer, many people learned of my interest in CmC and so I would daily find my reader full of E-mail, forums, or other documents in which CmC was even marginally referred to. Thus, people complain that they receive unsolicited files in their reader; some are useful and relevant, others are not.

Although time is not as urgent a factor as it is for E-messages, expert computer communicators avoid using more key strokes than absolutely necessary and so many of the conventions used in E-messages (e.g. "ur"; "what????") are also used in E-mail.

The dynamic, but ambiguous interpretation of silence has already been discussed for E-messages. In many instances, replies to E-mail may take days or weeks, even though most people respond to E-mail as soon as it arrives. The delay is taken as an indication that either the person is busy or does not have the relevant information and will respond when he/she does. Many users assume that the E-mail eventually arrives. However, as more non-technical people use E-mail, this assumption is changing. Managers and administrators need to know that the recipient actually receives the E-mail. Thus, many people use optional programs that tell the sender that the recipient saw the E-mail in his/her reader. This does not, of course, guarantee the E-mail was actually read or acted upon. It does, however, allow senders to say "you got my mail".

### 3.3 *Computer Conferencing*

Computer Conferencing refers to a facility in which more than two people can communicate with E-messages, E-mail and documents, usually for a specific purpose. Most computer conferencing facilities require all participants to be simultaneously logged on to the facility. Since the introduction of efficient fora, computer conferences are seldom used within the company. Jim and other employees have access to external conferencing facilities such as EIES, but Les does not.

### 3.4 *Forums*

Forums (Fora) refer to E-mail-type files (usually on one technical topic) with a wide distribution list to which a recipient can append another piece of information. In many instances, fora are used like conferences, except that they do not require simultaneous log on. Les is responsible for several fora and appends several others. Fora range from the IS THERE? FORUM to the USERFRIEND FORUM, both for the IBM PC. The former is used for simple requests for information such as "Is there a graphics package for the PC that will let me draw large braces?". Someone reading the forum who knows of a commercially available or an internally developed program that does this, will append the forum with the appropriate reference. Once the answer has been appended, the person responsible for maintaining this forum may remove both question and answer and add them to an appropriate forum. In this case, they would be added to the GRAPHICS FORUM. USERFRIEND forum is more theoretical. In this, people discuss the philosophy and psychology of user friendly hardware and software and also the technical bases for designing them.

### 3.5 *Bulletin Boards*

Bulletin Boards are similar to fora except that the topics under discussion are often more general and the organization less structured. These are not used in IBM but are popular elsewhere.

## 3.6 *Documents*

Documents include memos, the minutes of meetings, reports and technical papers, that have formatting controls designed for printing. They may be sent to recipients in hard copy (printout), the recipient may be sent a formatted copy for reading on-line, or the recipient may be sent an unformatted copy that may be read on-line or formatted and printed locally. This is the word processing function of the computer. The potential for immediate participation is restricted unless the sender is asking for feedback, in which case the recipient may append, annotate or otherwise comment on the document. Documents can also be constructed jointly and this is very common within IBM.

Like many project and organization managers, Les composes and produces most of his own documents, memos, etc. on-line and never has a secretary do this work.

More and more documents are read in soft copy only. The IBM telephone directory, for example, is now available both on-line and in hard copy. As on-line documents are becoming the standard, people's attitudes to hard copy are changing. Because of human subjects requirements for this study, I had to send out my questionnaire in hard copy for people to sign. I received many complaints, including some refusals to participate because it could not be completed on-line.

Manuals explaining the use of hardware and software are still largely provided in hard copy, allowing the user to consult the manual while carrying out the commands on the terminal. However, on-line help files are available for most programs and are often more useful than the manuals. Help files are usually menu-based. In one such instance, Mary has a problem with options available for the Park Lab printer; so, she types in the command (the name of the printer). On the screen, she sees a menu of printing options. Since she is interested in knowing what fonts are available, she can either type FONT in the command line or move the cursor to FONT on the menu and hit the enter key. She then reads a screen listing all the fonts she can choose. Some menus allow choices only by pressing the PF key assigned to the item.

Les reads very little in hard copy. He read this whole manuscript on-line, for example. Through years of practice, he can scan and read screens more quickly than he can read printed text.

## 3.7 *Bill Boards*

Bill Board refers to the on-line distribution of information. This can include schedules, cafeteria menus, and news. In general, most users can access bill boards to retrieve information, but not to insert information. Thus, the potential for immediate participation is restricted. A user could, for example, send E-mail or an E-message to the holder of the schedule and request an item be inserted, changed or deleted.

## 4. Hard copy

### 4.1 *Paper/print*

Paper/print is being used less and less within IBM. However, because of legal requirements, documents such as contracts have to be produced in hard copy. Initially, however, contracts are drawn up and negotiated on-line. Then, after legal approval, a hard copy is signed by the parties. By convention, manuals are still distributed in hard copy, although more and more, on-line HELP files are available. Agendas for meetings are usually distributed in hard copy at the beginning of a meeting. Hard copy handouts are usually given at meetings and presentations, allowing attendees to write notes on the handout during the meeting or presentation. Les often receives requests for information through E-mail. When he finds the information in a file, he may make brief notes to himself on scratch paper, indicating the files and disk, so he can put this into the E-mail he sends to the requestor. He does not use paper and pen for reminder notes on what he must do; rather he types this into a file and calls up the file when he wants to check work still outstanding.

Les and his colleagues fill out many forms in the course of a working year. These include purchase requests, requests for staff, and refunds for travel expenses. These forms are then submitted to the appropriate department either directly or through a secretary. Already several IBM organizations provide these forms on-line. A program automatically inserts information such as name, department code, etc. and the employee inserts the details specific to this request. The final record, however, is in hard copy.

Although many IBM employees regularly use both internal mail and the United States Postal Service, Les uses internal mail only three to four times a year and remembers using external mail only once in the last five years.

### 4.2 *Overhead transparencies*

Overhead transparencies (called foils in IBM) are used widely for presentations. Les produces these in an on-line file and then prints them on a special printer that has a wide range of fonts, including large print for foils. He then runs the print page through a transparency maker or a photocopier that takes transparencies. Les, like many other managers, produces his own foils and does not rely on secretarial help for this.

### 4.3 *Whiteboard*

Each office and meeting room has a whiteboard. Les often goes over to the whiteboard in his or a colleague's office to explain a technical point. In meetings, participants will get up from their chairs and explain a point using the whiteboard for listing or diagramming. Sometimes there will be more than one person at the whiteboard, each building on the other's explanations. Office whiteboards are also used as reminder boards.

# Chapter 4

# WHO SPEAKS TO WHOM

As we have seen in Chapter 3, Les and his colleagues have a variety of communication resources on which to draw. In this chapter, I will identify the networks of interaction in which Les participates, concentrating primarily on interactive CmC: E-mail and E-messages.

Over the initial eight-month observation period, Les communicated with 78 colleagues at 15 different IBM locations via E-messages and with 416 at 59 different locations via E-mail.

Formal definition of terms such as conversation is one of the goals of this study and will be discussed in Chapters 8 and 9. For the purposes of this chapter, I will make no distinction between complete and incomplete conversations. In order to quantify communications, I have used one piece of E-mail as the unit for communications via E-mail. For communication via E-messages I have used two different units: E-message and dialogue. E-message is not as formal a unit as E-mail because its length and therefore the number of E-messages are determined by the system, not the sender. Because I had access only to Les's console log, there is a further technical complication that results in the number of E-messages from Les not being formally equivalent to the number of E-messages to Les. When he types an E-message, he may type more than 80 characters. The system will automatically break up this line to fit the character limit. However, on his terminal and therefore in his log, this E-message appears as one E-message. The E-messages he receives, however, arrive and are recorded in their divided form. The following example illustrates this problem. Les received two E-messages from Peter. However, Peter typed this information as one line before he sent it to Les. Because the line was too long, the system broke it into two E-messages in the middle of the word "earlier" (Example 11). On Peter's log, however, this would appear as one E-message (Example 12).

```
(11) FROM MSNVM(PETER):   I MIGHT HAVE GUESSED (IN FACT I DID). I
                          WANT NOTHING – SHE SENT ME A MSG E
     FROM MSNVM(PETER):   ARLIER AND I WAS RESPONDING.
```

| | | |
|---|---|---|
| (12) | vmsg les | i might have guessed (in fact i did). i want nothing – she sent me a msg earlier and i was responding |

An E-message count will be therefore biased towards Les sending fewer than his interactants. Therefore, I have also used dialogue as a unit of measurement. A dialogue refers to any series of E-messages that make a unit because there is no further communication on the same subject the same day or, if there is, this second communication is introduced by an opening or topic shift marker. However, if the E-messages are contiguous, they are classified as one dialogue, even if there is a topic shift.

| | | |
|---|---|---|
| (13) | vmsg elmvm(ted) | i can't find the pid maclibs on the cms/sp3 source disks |
| | vmsg elmvm(ted) | in building A . . . everything else appears to be there |
| | FROM ELMVM(TED): | . . they're on cmssp 3 290 (pid) disk |
| | FROM ELMVM(TED): | . . ac 290 xx/xx * maclib |
| | vmsg elmvm(ted) | ok, doing the first pass at the send assembles |
| | vmsg elmvm(ted) | soon as that is working, will convert rest of send updates |
| | vmsg elmvm(ted) | . . . btw, is there any project on elmvm1 |
| | FROM ELMVM(TED): | . . Project? |
| | FROM ELMVM(TED): | . . Currently, it is down (Hardware problem) |
| | FROM ELMVM(TED): | . . They say it'll be up at 4, but I don't believe it. |
| | FROM ELMVM(TED): | . . Did you send the Friday Message? |

Les then went to E-mail and sent information concerning a Friday meeting to several colleagues. He used E-mail because it went to a long distribution list.

This dialogue has three topics: where the maclib is; whether there is a project on ELMVM1; and whether Les had sent a message about a Friday meeting. However, I have classified it as one dialogue because these E-messages are contiguous.

## 1. Networks of dialogues via E-messages

As would be expected, most of Les's dialogues (as defined earlier) were with colleagues at the five Labs involved in his projects: Park, El Monte, Mission, Pippin and Bermuda (see Figure 1). However, these dialogues were not all related to his projects or to the products for which he is responsible. Often, colleagues requested more general information, drawing on Les's technical expertise. In addition, several dialogues relate to organizational planning such as arranging for meetings.

Figure 1. *Dialogues per location*[11]

| *Location* | *Number of interactants* | *Number of dialogues* |
|---|---|---|
| PARK | 13 | 196 |
| ELMONTE | 29 | 119 |
| MISSION | 5 | 54 |
| PIPPIN | 13 | 47 |
| BERMUDA | 4 | 9 |
| SWEDEN | 1 | 4 |
| East Coast 1 | 3 | 4 |
| FRANCE | 2 | 2 |
| West Coast 1 | 2 | 2 |
| East Coast 2 | 1 | 2 |
| Other US 1 | 1 | 1 |
| East Coast 3 | 1 | 1 |
| Other US 2 | 1 | 1 |
| West Coast 2 | 1 | 1 |
| West Coast 3 | 1 | 1 |

Over the eight-month initial observation period, Les participated in 442 dialogues, of which he initiated only 26%. These dialogues consisted of a total of 2801 E-messages, 1302 of which Les sent. As noted above, this figure is probably lower because my data show Les's E-messages as typed in, rather than as split by the system. However, these figures do indicate that, although Les initiates only 26% of the dialogues, he provides at least 50% of the E-messages. Of his 78 interactants, only 11 had more than 10 dialogues with Les (set out in Figure 2 with their location).

Figure 2. *Dialogues per interactant*

| *Interactant* | *Number of conversations* | *Les initiated* |
|---|---|---|
| DON (Park) | 54 | 13 |
| SIMON (Park) | 52 | 13 |
| BRIAN (Park) | 37 | 13 |
| PETER (Mission) | 25 | 1 |
| MAT (Mission) | 20 | 4 |
| JIM (El Monte) | 21 | 1 |
| MARY (Park) | 19 | 4 |
| JOHN (Park) | 18 | 3 |
| JOHND (El Monte) | 18 | 1 |
| ROBERT (Pippin) | 15 | 4 |
| GORDON (Pippin) | 11 | 4 |

These interactants are either at the same location as Les or directly involved in supporting his projects. The only exception is JohnD, who is the local PC expert and who is a major interactant (both through E-messages and E-mail), because he provides Les with information concerning new PC software and hardware; his role explains why he initiates 17 of the 18 dialogues.

**2. Networks of dialogues via E-mail**

As indicated above, the unit here is one E-mail file. Consequently the numbers appear very large, in comparison to those for E-messages. However, the major interactants change. Al, Sid and several others (Lisa from New York) become more important than those more local interactants. These interactants are marked with an *. Figure 3 lists all the interactants identified as major E-message interactants and any who have sent and received more than 50 pieces of E-mail in conversations with Les.

Figure 3. *E-Mail per interactant*

| *Interactant* | *Total pieces of E-mail* | *E-mail sent by Les* |
|---|---|---|
| JIM (El Monte) | 264 | 130 |
| DAVE (El Monte)* | 146 | 69 |
| AL (Pippin)* | 155 | 87 |
| SIMON (Park) | 124 | 74 |
| SID (Bermuda)* | 114 | 54 |
| JOHN (Park) | 106 | 48 |
| GORDON (Pippin) | 105 | 96 |
| ROBERT (Pippin) | 91 | 63 |
| MIKE (Bermuda)* | 86 | 42 |
| LISA (New York)* | 84 | 39 |
| BRIAN (Park) | 83 | 41 |
| TED (El Monte)* | 69 | 53 |
| MARK (El Monte)* | 65 | 37 |
| JOHND (El Monte) | 62 | 23 |
| MAT (Mission) | 58 | 21 |
| PETER (Mission) | 47 | 21 |
| DON (Park) | 41 | 21 |
| MARY (Park) | 24 | 5 |

Several colleagues become major interactants because they are system programmers at the locations where Les has USERIDs or project contacts. Dave and Mark are system programmers at El Monte Lab, and Mike is a system programmer at Bermuda Lab.

As we shall see in Chapter 5, most computer users have personal preferences for particular modes of communication (which I call conversational style). Sid, for example, rarely engages in conversations via E-messages. He and Les had only four dialogues, all of which were initiated by Sid. Three were requests for Les to telephone and the remaining one was a brief question to which Les responded with a brief reply. Sid's preferred mode is the telephone.

Lisa and Les correspond often using E-mail, yet they have no E-message dialogues. She does sometimes call Les. Lisa is the administrative manager directly responsible for allocating funds and organizing contracts for Projects SEND and FALCON. Her preferred mode of communication is E-mail.

Al is a director of Project SEND and mainly communicates with Les via E-mail or face-to-face conversation. Don, on the other hand, prefers E-messages to E-mail.

## 3. Carbon Copying (CC)

As noted in Chapter 3, sending E-mail to several people is very simple with the computer. Much of the E-mail listed in Figure 3 was sent to more than one person, as shown in Figure 4. Figure 4 is listed in the same order as Figure 3, from the largest number of pieces of E-mail to the smallest.

There is considerable difference in the number of E-mail items Les sends only to the individual and the numbers sent to several people. Most E-mail he sends to Lisa is sent only to her because it involves funding and contracts that have to be worked out between the two of them. Most of Les's E-mail to John, however, is also sent to other colleagues. John's data center supports Les's projects and so, out of courtesy, Les informs him of decisions made or suggestions proposed. Similarly, most of Les's E-mail to his manager is sent only to Gordon because Les is asking his advice and help on his projects or giving him updates.

Les interacts with 416 colleagues both in the United States and around the world via E-mail. The number of colleagues and their locations appear in Figure 5.

## 4. Networks of dialogues via telephone

Les engages in about 7 telephone conversations each day. His interactants fall into 3 groups:

- colleagues within IBM who prefer the telephone,
- colleagues within IBM who have not received a reply to CmC,

Figure 4. *Carbon Copy E-Mail per interactant*

| Inter-actant | E-mail sent by Les (no CC) | E-mail sent CC by Les | E-mail sent by X (no CC) | E-mail sent CC by X |
|---|---|---|---|---|
| JIM | 59 | 71 | 64 | 70 |
| DAVE* | 49 | 20 | 45 | 32 |
| AL* | 61 | 26 | 65 | 3 |
| SIMON | 32 | 42 | 44 | 6 |
| SID* | 23 | 31 | 47 | 13 |
| JOHN | 12 | 36 | 39 | 19 |
| GORDON | 77 | 19 | 9 | 0 |
| ROBERT | 28 | 35 | 20 | 8 |
| MIKE* | 24 | 18 | 33 | 11 |
| LISA* | 33 | 6 | 35 | 10 |
| BRIAN | 21 | 20 | 37 | 5 |
| TED* | 20 | 33 | 12 | 4 |
| MARK* | 1 | 36 | 4 | 24 |
| JOHND | 15 | 8 | 19 | 20 |
| MAT | 8 | 13 | 25 | 12 |
| PETER | 9 | 12 | 14 | 12 |
| DON | 4 | 17 | 10 | 10 |
| MARY | 5 | 0 | 15 | 4 |

– colleagues outside IBM not tied into the computer network.
This latter group can also be divided into three groups:
– employees of NEWS and BASC,
– former IBM employees,
– merchants supplying hardware.
NEWS and BASC are the two companies providing hardware for Projects SEND and FALCON. These companies are not tied into the computer network and so Les must contact them via the telephone or in face-to-face meetings. Les maintains contact with several former IBM employees and friends who, because of their current positions, are able to help Les with information on products (both software and hardware) available outside IBM. One of Les's projects involves the IBM PC and Les has contacted several local merchants to get software and hardware for his PCs.

## 5. Networks of dialogues via face-to-face interaction

Les travels to the East Coast twice a month to have meetings with his project teams at Pippin and Bermuda Labs. During these visits, he may also make

Figure 5. *Interactants per location*

| Location | | Interactants |
|---|---|---|
| WEST COAST: | Park | 2 |
| | Elmonte | 81 |
| | Mission | 14 |
| | other | 46 |
| NEW YORK STATE: | Pippin | 46 |
| | Bermuda | 28 |
| | Stanton | 30 |
| | other | 37 |
| OTHER US STATES | | 64 |
| CANADA | | 8 |
| EUROPE: | England | 15 |
| | France | 4 |
| | Germany | 4 |
| | Holland | 6 |
| | Denmark, Italy | 1ea. |
| | Sweden, Switzerland | 1ea. |
| ASIA/PACIFIC/AFRICA: | Australia | 1 |
| | Singapore | 1 |
| | Japan | 3 |
| | South Africa | 1 |

presentations to a large number of interested colleagues. Also, he makes chance encounters in the corridors and over coffee or lunch. Al, Sandy, Robert and Sid also often visit the West Coast to have both formal and informal meetings with Les and his colleagues in California. Locally, he has formal meetings with colleagues from Park, El Monte and Mission Labs. He often visits these other labs and has informal encounters with colleagues there. He also meets several colleagues at a local cafe. Les also makes presentations at IBM organized conferences and so interacts with a large number of colleagues from around the world.

# Chapter 5

# WHO SPEAKS WHAT LANGUAGE TO WHOM AND WHEN?[12]

In interviews and during informal conversations over lunch or in the hallways, Les and his colleagues often commented on their use of CmC and discussed, sometimes heatedly, the relative merits of available modes of communication. Many comments concerned the actual implementation of these tools, rather than an ideal version of the mode. Since such implementations do affect the way people use the available modes of communication, in this chapter, I will use quotations from interview transcriptions and field notes to compare and illustrate users' views (and explanations which often accompanied the quotations cited from interviews) with observations of actual uses of communication modes.

"*I'm not sure the person actually gets the message.*" Before Les sends messages, like most of his colleagues, he checks first to see if the intended recipient is logged on. To do this, he uses a program which checks the USERID of the person he wants to communicate with. If he wants to talk with Peter, for example, he looks for him on-line and the system sends back one of four possible replies:

1. PETER NOT LOGGED ON
2. PETER – DSC
3. PETER – 4zz
4. PETER – L01

1 means Peter is not logged on. 2 means he has disconnected, possibly leaving a GONE message. Both 3 and 4 indicate that he is logged on. 3 indicates the number identity of the terminal at MSNVM at which he is logged on, while 4 indicates that he is logged on remotely, either from home or another IBM location. When Les receives the NOT LOGGED ON or DSC reply, he may send E-mail or a file, knowing Peter will receive it when he next logs on. However, if he wants to communicate urgently with Peter and receives the DSC reply, he sends a quick message so he will receive the GONE reply Peter has typed in. He then knows where Peter is and when he will be able to contact him

via E-messages or the telephone. The usual convention for doing this is to send the message "hi" since it requires few key strokes, but, if the person has returned, does not appear odd or rude. If Les gets the reply that Peter is logged on, he can send E-mail or a file or an E-message. In the latter case, however, like many of his colleagues, he often checks first to see if Peter is actually at his terminal and is willing to engage in an E-message conversation. The convention for this summons is usually "you there?" since it requires few key strokes, but requests a reply. If Peter is not actually at his terminal, Les does not want to send an E-message because it will probably be lost. Peter might be at his terminal but might not want to communicate: he might be very busy with other work or may be working at his terminal with another colleague and not want potentially confidential information coming on the screen.

"*I don't want sensitive E-messages left on the screen*." During my visit to Pippin Lab, Susan told me of an incident which has made her even more careful than most when sending E-messages. She was teaching an IBM class how to use a word processing program. To do this, she uses her own USERID and terminal and has the screen projected onto a large screen in the room so everyone can see it. She was in the middle of explaining a particular point when an E-message flashed across the screen from Robert, asking her opinion of an especially sensitive meeting held that morning. She immediately sent Robert an E-message telling him she was in class and using her terminal screen for teaching purposes. She says she is now much more careful about using the NOT RECEIVING option when in class and always sends a summons E-message (e.g. "hi" or "you there?") herself to people before sending any real information.

The choice of NOT RECEIVING can be a nuisance, however, as can be seen in the following situation. Mary and Susan had sent several pieces of E-mail to each other. Mary sent E-mail and, as soon as it went over the network, realized she had forgotten one small point. She knew Susan was logged on because she had just received E-mail from her. Thus, she sent a quick one-line E-message. She then got back the system E-message that Susan was NOT RECEIVING, went into E-mail, explained to Susan that she'd just sent an E-message and repeated the E-message.

Another way people deal with sensitive E-messages is to use a different mode, as can be seen in the following example. Mary has asked several people at the El Monte Research Lab to cooperate with her in her research project. Most have expressed willingness, but a couple have said they want management approval for their cooperation. She tells John, her manager, and Stuart, her project manager, through E-mail. She then goes out of town for several days. On her return, after reading E-mail from Stuart telling her he has not received objections from anyone concerning her project, she begins E-mail to him to ask what she should do next, when John initiates the following dialogue:

(14) J1: WELCOME BACK!
J2: GIME A SHOUT WHEN YOU HAVE SOME TIME . . . I HAVE SOME INTERESTING FEEDBACK TO SHARE WITH YOU. . .
J3: FROM OUR NEAT-O "FRIENDS".
M1: yep, right now – was just sending a note to stuart on same subject.
J4: OK, I'LL HEAD DOWN TO YOUR OFFICE.

John chose face-to-face communication because the topic was extremely sensitive, involving reporting what he had been told by a third party. It was not gossip because it was a report on why Mary's colleagues at the El Monte Lab had not yet been given clearance to participate in her project. However, he did not want the third party to be implicated and wanted to be sure that Mary fully understood the delicacy of the situation. He chose face-to-face so 1) it could not be overheard and 2) all the paralinguistic cues were available for him to present his case and be able to ensure that Mary had interpreted the information as intended. Mary, John and Stuart agree not to pursue the matter for a while. Some weeks later, John is told that Mary has management approval and can have the help of people at the El Monte Lab for her research.

"*getting into synch mode of operation. typing is slower than speaking.*" Les's manager, Gordon, sends him an E-message

(15a) FROM PIPPVM(GORDON): ARE YOU THERE TONIGHT?

Then follows the exchange of E-messages discussing technical and personnel details concerning projects SEND and FALCON. After 40 E-messages, Les says:

(15b) vmsg pippvm (gordon) i'm going to call, just a moment

Les said later that they had got "in synch" and so a telephone call was more efficient. By this, he means that he and Gordon had become completely focused on their conversation and were no longer doing any parallel work. Les and Gordon were both waiting for a response before sending their next E-message. Although they are both touch typists, computer messaging is still slower than an oral conversation.

One-finger typists have an even greater motivation to cut short potentially lengthy E-message dialogues. Guy sends a simple request to Les and expects a one-line answer. Instead, Les begins responding with a series of "what if . . ." statements which Guy responds to. After 9 E-messages (a short interaction in comparison to the 40 in Les's dialogue with Gordon) Guy sends the following E-message:

(15c) MSG FROM GUY: Fingers wearing out, what's your number?

"*it's (E-message) usually one-liners ... isn't extensive amount of explanation involved.*" If the topic is a quick, simple request for information, an E-message is most likely to be chosen because it does not interrupt any other work, as in the following two examples.

(16a) Simon: has Campbell sent you the OOPS module?

(16b) Guy: I DON'T HAVE A 370 PRINC OF OPS.

"*very detailed long explanations ... more suited to the note file (E-mail).*" In his interview on this point, Les continued "if it involves a detailed technical discussion. There is a current one going on where somebody made a complex statement of the inner workings of the CP algorithm and lead up to it by making several general statements and then making the assertion that if something was changed in the following way, that would be more conducive based on his general impression of the way things worked. In replying to that, attempting to point out that things weren't exactly like the person believed it was—the amount of information involved in his original statement was two or three hundred words and included a half a dozen facts and it was hard to answer that. It required switching back and forth between what the original statement was to make sure all the bases were covered." He used E-mail for his response because it allowed him to move back and forth between the original question and his response.

In another situation, Simon asked Les for advice on how to fix a particular bug. Les sent screens full of information on this highly technical point. He then learned that both Simon and another system programmer who was having similar problems were both in Simon's office. Les stopped typing E-messages and went to Simon's office where he explained what he had sent as E-messages. When asked why he had done this, he said he "wanted to be sure they had really understood as it was a complex problem. I had to use the whiteboard to explain."

"*the telephone interrupts. It predisposes you to be surly because it's sure to be a problem. The solution demands immediate response.*" CmC is chosen for requests for action, often in preference to face-to-face or telephone conversations. Participants do not need to spend time on social maintenance conversations and they can be sure the recipient will get the correct E-message. Many managers prefer E-mail and E-messages to the telephone because a telephone call often results only in leaving a message with a secretary asking the recipient to call back. The recipient calls back but the sender is out and a message is left with his/her secretary. Such attempts to communicate often lead to secretaries talking to each other and the managers never making contact. This situation is so common, it is frequently referred to as "telephone tag". With CmC (especially E-mail), the sender knows the recipient will be able to read the E-mail and respond as soon as s/he logs on.

"*you never know who's going to read it.*" Users assign their communications to specific people and groups of people. However, since distribution of other people's E-mail is simple with a computer, there is always the possibility that a piece of E-mail intended for one person may be distributed to others. Users will thus often switch from E-mail to face-to-face or telephone if they do not want the information passed on. Other communicators place a "For Your Eyes Only" statement at the top of the E-mail and rely on the recipient to abide by this request.

When a request for information comes in E-mail, the recipient will respond with E-mail to that one person. However, since the problem may have affected many people who also send requests for the same information, the recipient may then distribute the same E-mail to others. The problem may prove to be so general that the E-mail is appended to an appropriate forum for an even wider distribution. Or, the problem may require negotiation and a complete change of medium is made, to a meeting, for example.

"*I don't know how he'd construe that . . . the nature of the medium (computer) is constricted. Can't really tell what people mean.*" In the following example Peter switches medium so Ted does know what he means because there is a possible confusion between institutional power and personal power. Peter and his system programmer, Ted, who are also personal friends, are involved in a lengthy computer conversation via E-messages, which results in a disagreement over manuals to help users. Rather than continue with E-messages, Peter sends Ted the following E-message:

(17) please call – we've *got* to discuss. call me when you get to work.

In this conversation, Peter and Ted are negotiating roles. Earlier in the same interaction, Peter questioned why Ted had installed a new system before completely debugging it. He expressed annoyance first, by typing "humpf" and later, by responding "sigh", when Ted indicated that he had not installed all the necessary access codes. After more computer-mediated discussion that did not resolve the problems, Peter requests a phone call. If he had continued to press for more documentation through E-messages, Ted might have construed it as Peter enforcing his institutional role of manager, which he did not want to do. He felt that in a telephone call he could more easily establish equal role status, especially through the use of intonation.

Other researchers (Kiesler, Siegel and McGuire 1984) have identified a phenomenon they call flaming. They claim that participants in CmC are less inhibited than in face-to-face dialogues and use more emotive and inflammatory language. They attribute this freedom of expression to the lack of visual and aural cues and that appenders to conferences have no awareness of audience. This is not borne out in the study reported here—either in E-messages, E-mail or conferences. While there is very direct use of language, there is little evidence of vulgar words. More importantly, when compared with face-to-face interactions, the same people tend to use the same language and some even temper their language in CmC. In later discussions with participants, they have reported that they would probably have used "stronger" language had the dialogue been face-to-face. Brian suggested this is "because you never know who's going to read it. I assume it will be copied and sent to some other person". Another colleague suggested that flaming was a sign of "novices, immature computer users, not computer professionals".

The Kiesler, Siegel and McGuire study has attracted media attention and been reported in newspapers and magazines. This research was reported and discussed in several IBM fora, giving rise to the suggested use of icons to cover all possible human feelings (referred to in Chapter 3).

"*my husband and I met and got to know each other over ARPANET.*"[13] While there is ample evidence for relationships being developed through traditional letters or on-line, if people have not had any previous contact, they will often choose a channel-rich medium to establish the initial relationship. In the following example, Mary had sent a file to Guy requesting feedback on the information it contained. G1 is Guy's response to this request through E-mail. M1 was also sent as E-mail and G2 as an E-message. Mary sent an E-message the following day to say she was in her office and Guy could call at his convenience. He called within five minutes of receiving the E-message and Mary and Guy had a telephone conversation for about 1 hour. Mary asked Guy why he wanted to talk on the phone rather than through computer communication. He replied that since they had never met or communicated before, he wanted to get a "feel" for who she was which, he felt, could best be done with a rich medium.

(18) G1: Mary,
I have glanced at the QUESTION file. What phone number should I call to reach you?
M1: My phone number is: tie-line 273-4180

outside line 997-4180
G2: When is a good time to call you?

*"most (people) rather send E-mail than E-messages. It's more permanent."* During a conversation with Brian in his office, Les told Brian of source files available on his system but not on Brian's. He got a listing of the necessary files on his screen and then wrote these into computer E-mail to Brian, who was standing beside him. The file names had numbers and letter mixes and were not easily remembered. Thus, Les chose to commit these to a more permanent medium so Brian would not have to remember them and risk making an error.

*"It's a problem to respond on the fly." "E-mail gives you more time to think."* Computer communicators cite examples where they choose computer E-mail for a logically, well-argued statement, which is then followed by a telephone call or face-to-face conversation. This removes personal and emotional issues from the initial discussion that might result if there were maximum potential for participation by the receiver. Further, some users suggest they use computer E-messages because they are unplanned and have few established conventions. Thus, they can "get away with" things they would not be able to say elsewhere.

*"The terminal can provide an integrated work environment. Person may be able to multiplex ... to manage simultaneous activities."* In fact, because of the time delays and the lack of need to keep eye contact or provide back channel cues, Les is able to do a variety of other work while engaged in a computer conversation (see opening vignette in Chapter 2). This other work can include telephone conversations, technical work, word processing, face-to-face conversation, and other computer conversations.

Computer users often choose computer conversation in preference to telephone conversation, because they can do other work at the same time. For them, the computer is less interruptive than the telephone. However, others find computer conversations also disruptive because they have to interrupt the work they are currently doing. The choice depends largely on two factors: number of terminals and the nature of the other work being done. In Les's case, E-messages are especially non-disruptive because he has two terminals and can carry on the conversation on one and do technical or word-processing work on the other. If workers are running a program, they are not interrupted by E-messages. However, if they are word processing or doing some other applications, they must move back and forth between the application and the E-message conversation. In such cases, E-messages are most disruptive.

"*It frees you from time zone.*" "*out of joint—Europe—ongoing conversation but work hours not overlap so immediate messages (E-messages) not possible.*" Les usually sends E-mail to a colleague in Australia. He may send an E-message if they are logged on at the same time, but this is very rare because of the time difference. Stuart, on the other hand, sends E-mail to a colleague in Chile because the telephone lines are unreliable.

"*at least when he's here you can pin him down and talk.*" "*it's a real pain to converse with Martin. He always uses E-mail and it takes so much more time and interrupts.*" Some of Les's colleagues never use E-messages, preferring to speak on the telephone. Sid often sends one-liners asking Les to call. On one occasion, he said:

(19) MSG FROM SID : ONE CALL WORTH 1000 WORDS 9-999-9999

People in fact have preferred modes. Al prefers to talk to Les face-to-face so he "can pin him down". Sid prefers to call. Martin prefers to send E-mail. These preferences are similar to the notion of conversational style Tannen (1984) has identified in face-to-face conversations. Since conversational styles and mode and medium preferences differ among people and among different groups, the possiblity for misunderstanding, or even conflict, exists. Thus, Peter considers it a "pain" to converse with Martin via computers since he will use only E-mail and not E-messages, even for short one-line requests or responses, while some of Les's interactants consider him "remote" or "unresponsive" since he prefers to use CmC and does not always reply as promptly as they want or with the answer they want.

"*It just blows my mind that you have been forced by customs/legalities to ship pieces of cellulose back and forth all over the world to do a survey on ELECTRONIC MAIL!!!*" The above comment was sent to me as a result of my sending out the questionnaires as part of this study in hard copy so they could be signed to meet the informed consent regulation for studies of human subjects.

While all the previous comments are part of a cultural system of language use, there are culturally accepted conventions which are institutionalized: research reports always appear formatted for print (either on-line or hard copy); contracts are always in written form (currently hard copy only); presentations are always accompanied by foils (print or hand writing) and sometimes by hand outs (hard copy). We are in the process of witnessing changes in many of these formal conventions. Already, research reports and other documents are exchanged in soft copy but are still often filed in hard copy as well. Contracts are built and completed initially on-line. However, since the final contract is a legal document, it is always in hard copy because of the need for a legally binding signature. This will change very soon as work on on-line authorization develops a secure method of identification and a legal precedent is set for its use. As the technology develops, we will see further changes in current formal conventions. Within other institutions, conventions will change with the introduction of CmC. For example, we may soon see dissertations presented (and maybe even defended) on-line, just as we are seeing more and more publishers requesting soft copies of manuscripts.

"*a lot of it (CmC) is primarily related to working.*" I participated in many lunchtime conversations that included chat, talk about movies, cars, football, etc. in which people related incidents to each other. While the computer-mediated data do include topics not directly related to work, they include only two examples of relating of incidents, or what could be called chat. Phatic communication (first used by Malinowski 1923) identifies that part of our speech behavior used for social politeness and whose meaning is almost completely irrelevant. Phatic communication includes inquiries about health, comments on weather, and greetings. The actual meaning may be irrelevant, but the absence (and therefore presence) of such institutionalized items indicates meaning on the social plane of interaction. Phatic communication, then, focuses on social aspects rather than on action. In the data reported here, phatic communication rarely occurs by itself, but rather as an opening or closing to an action interchange such as

WELCOME BACK!
HAVE A NICE DAY.
Greetings, Bob

Colleagues do not usually greet each other when they log on. They do not exchange pleasantries such as "hi, how're things?" as they do when face-to-face, unless they are opening specific requests. When people are logged on from home at the weekend, they sometimes do begin a general interaction with "hi, what are you doing?"

We have now seen "Who uses what language to whom and when?" within this IBM VM community. Parts II and III will explore particular language use in more detail, specifically a taxonomy of the choices of mode and medium and a model of the discourse structure typical in CmC.

# PART II:

# TERMINAL LITERACY

The first characteristic of E-mail and E-messages that strikes the novice user is that it is a hybrid of both oral and written language. Earlier studies have drawn attention to this phenomenon (Levodow 1980; Conklin 1984; Murray 1985, 1988), identifying characteristics that can be attributed to the interactive nature of these modes or to their composed and edited aspect, that is, certain characteristics can be attributed to either an oral or a written style. This section takes the notion of oral and written style one step further by examining how Les and his colleagues make use of the range of different media resources available to them. "Adequate descriptions of literacy must include not only rules-of-use regarding the spoken and written codes but also rules-of-use involved in 'switching' back and forth between spoken and written language modes" (Nystrand 1982:11). Part II addresses this second issue. Chapter 6 discusses different models from a variety of disciplines, models that have sought to explain language variation and then proposes a framework for examining these data to answer the question Who speaks what language to whom and when? Chapter 7 provides a taxonomy of choices involved in using a particular medium or mode for communication.

# Chapter 6

# APPROACHES TO VARIATION IN LANGUAGE

> *More than anything, language is an activity motivated by users' needs to make things known in particular ways for particular purposes and to establish and maintain common understandings with other conversants; and the form of a particular text is always determined as much by the conversants' need to function in these situations as it is by whatever it is they wish to express.* (Nystrand 1982:10)

The study of variation in discourse spans many different disciplines and orientations: linguistics, anthropology, education, sociology, and philosophy. Anthropologists are primarily concerned with the function of the discourse in the culture; computational linguists are concerned with developing operational models of text production and understanding, usually within a narrow context; ethnomethodologists are concerned with developing rules for the organization of oral conversation; some literacy scholars are concerned with linking literacy to social practices. To meet varied goals, methods of analysis and underlying assumptions also vary. Anthropologists use a global approach to the analysis of naturally occurring data; computational linguists use an interpretive approach to prototypical texts; ethnomethodologists record short stretches of naturally occurring speech and subject them to detailed analysis; certain literacy scholars use historical or ethnographic data to look for recurring patterns of literacy practices.

As a result of these different perspectives, different terms have been used to account for variation: written/oral, ways of speaking, dialect, idiolect, style, register and genre. These terms both overlap and are complementary; none accounts for all aspects of language variation. I shall examine several traditions of research on oral and written language and then propose a framework for explaining the variation in language use demonstrated in Chapter 5.

## 1. Literacy traditions

Ong's (1977:42) view that "technology ... transforms what can be said and what is said" is not new. Since Aristotle, scholars have questioned the nature and value of new technologies of communication, technologies such as writing and print. Traditional views posited a dichotomy between orality and literacy, with acquisition of literacy changing the way people think. Plato in the Phaedrus (323) has Socrates point out that writing might weaken memory and writers might have the show of wisdom without the reality (cited in Scribner and Cole 1981:5). Similarly, scholars such as Hieronimo Squarciafico bemoaned the advent of print because it might destroy memory and weaken the mind (cited in Ong 1982:80). More recently, Goody and Watt (1968), for example, hypothesize that literacy reshapes consciousness while Eisenstein (1979), using historical data, shows how print affected society and made the modernization process possible. The effects that print and electronic media might have on consciousness received popular attention when McLuhan (1962, 1964) claimed that "the medium is the message". However, certain types of consciousness may be antecedent to literacy rather than a consequence of literacy (Olson 1977; Heath and Thomas 1984; Pattison 1982; Street 1984), a view that challenges the direct causal view of previous scholars. Although the relationship between thought and writing or thought and print is still unresolved, most researchers agree that certain uses of language co-occur with literacy and yet others co-occur with print or other technologies linked to writing.

Parallel with the traditional view that literacy changes consciousness is the view that oral and written language are dichotomous: writing is the suitable vehicle for rational, critical thinking (Goody 1968); writing is analytic and sequential (Ong 1977); meaning and authority are lodged "in the text" (Olson 1981); oral language is personal and emotional (Goody 1968); oral language is formulaic (Ong 1982); spoken discourse is context-bound. Most discussion of academic writing and literacy (for example Ong 1982 and Olson 1981) refers to the necessity of divorcing the author from the text. "Meaning and the authority are displaced from the intentions of a speaker and lodged 'in the text'" (Olson 1981:110). Research into the differences between listening and reading (for example, Hildyard and Olson 1978) has shown that listeners listen to what the discourse means whereas readers concentrate and remember the actual written words. In effect, all these researchers and theorists claim that orality and literacy are two different ways of viewing and dealing with the world; certain ways of thinking are only possible through the written word.

This dichotomous view is disputed by recent researchers who suggest instead an oral/literate continuum (for example, Tannen 1982). Many of these studies (for example, Chafe 1982) have examined academic writing and dinnertable conversations as representative of two maximally differentiated styles on the oral-literate continuum and have then identified certain strategies as those most likely to be associated with orality contrasted with those most likely to be associated with literacy. One such strategy is the amount of planning. Because speaking is faster than writing, it is less planned (for example, Chafe 1982; Halliday 1985), as evidenced by the integrative nature of writing, contrasted with the fragmentary nature of speaking. Chafe examined his academic writing and dinnertable conversation data for discourse features that realize these characteristics. Such features include presence of nominalization and complement clauses as realizations of integration. While spontaneity and planning are related to oral and written discourse respectively, as Lakoff (1982) points out, they should not be directly equated since there is non-spontaneous oral discourse and spontaneous written discourse. However, such discourse is considered untypical of oral and written discourse.

A second difference claimed between speaking and writing is that speakers interact directly with their audiences while writers do not. This speaker interaction has been characterized as personal involvement (Chafe 1982), which is realized through surface manifestations such as fuzziness and first-person reference. More recently, Tannen (1985) has developed Chafe's notion of personal involvement, claiming that strategies associated with orality grow out of focus on personal involvement of speaker and writer whereas strategies associated with literacy grow out of focus on content. Another researcher, Bell (1984), reaches a similar conclusion, claiming that style shift results from audience design, by which he means that changes in language style result from changes in audience. Speakers and writers design their language to suit their audience. While this is also a common theme in composition and literary studies, the data presented in this book clearly indicate that such a claim oversimplifies the complex interaction between language choice and various aspects of the context; not all shifts can be attributed to audience.

Both the traditional and continuum views of literacy begin with the assumption that a stretch of discourse is either written or oral, rather than by considering different discourse samples as part of the linguistic repertoire of the speech community. It is this assumption (which I will show is false) that then leads scholars to claim that it is whether a stretch of discourse is spoken or written that determines its characteristics. Heath (1983) and Street (1984) do accept different literacies as social products practiced within a community, but do not situate these literacies within a sociolinguistic model, which I shall attempt to do here. By taking language use (or contextual factors) rather than form as my starting point, I found that medium represents part of the meaning potential (Halliday 1973) available to language users; available media are options from which speakers choose (not necessarily consciously) in the same way they make other linguistic choices, choices that depend on the context of situation (Halliday 1973).

## 2. Ways of speaking

Ways of speaking (Hymes 1972) is a general term that covers variation within a community. As an anthropologist, Hymes called for "socially constituted linguistics" in which "the object of linguistic study is:

1. The organization of linguistic features within a speech community in terms of ways of speaking within a verbal repertoire.
2. Membership in a speech community in which individuals share one (or more) ways of speaking" (p. 319).

These "ways of speaking" may be regarded as both rules of co-occurrence and rules of alternation (Ervin-Tripp 1972). The former determine the way in which a speech community selects and bundles linguistic features from its repertoire while the latter relate speech styles to context.

Because CmC is a recent phenomenon, with few established conventions, and because it appears a hybrid of both oral and written language (Levodow 1980; Conklin 1984; Murray 1985, 1988), it illustrates how a speech community adapts a new medium to its repertoire of communication media and, in particular, how the community makes choices among the available modes and media. This study shows the need for finer specifications of the dimensions involved in this choice than have been described in models (for example, Malinowski 1923; Firth 1957; Jakobson 1960; Hymes 1972; Halliday 1973) that seek to identify "Who speaks what language to whom and when?" (Fishman 1965), an enterprise Hymes and others call the ethnography of speaking. I will discuss some of the ways in which different scholars have sought to describe and explain the interaction between language form and use, including speech style, register and genre all of which have been identified with such "ways of speaking".

### 2.1 *Speech style*

Speech style[14] has been used primarily by anthropologists and linguists influenced by Hymes (see, for example, Irvine 1982, Urban 1982 and Tannen 1984). The fundamental question is whether it is used to describe individual or social group variation. For Sapir (in Mandelbaum 1949:542), style is "an everyday facet of speech that characterizes both social group and the individual" whereas for Tannen (1984) and Urban (1982) style refers only to individual ways of speaking. Bell (1984) uses style to refer to intraspeaker variation but claims it has its roots in interspeaker variation. He considers audience design as the single most important factor accounting for variation in language. While admitting that content and setting are important, he claims that variation is a result of what the speaker thinks the audience knows or needs to know about the content or setting. Like literacy scholars who have taken medium as given, Bell takes content and other aspects of setting also as given.

In anthropology, speech style has been associated with speech events, the events a community considers salient and outside observers note as salient. These are defined by the fact that the type of language used is different from what precedes and what follows. However, speech style and register are used almost synonymously by Hymes (1972), because both refer to a kind of language, not a unit of discourse structure (genre).

## 2.2 *Register*

Register differs from dialect or sociolect because it is a "variety according to use" rather than a "variety according to user" (Halliday et al. 1964:77). Register variation has been studied primarily by British linguists and applied linguists influenced by systemic linguistics (see, for example, Gregory 1967; Ellis and Ure 1969; Gibbon 1981; Ventola 1985). Their discussions have focused on constructing taxonomies of the parameters influencing register, such as field, mode and participants. Other researchers have used register as a useful label for intuitively recognizable kinds of language (for example, Henzl 1974; Haviland 1979; Ferguson 1977, 1983). Scholars who use register for interpersonal and intrapersonal language variation retain style for the more specific variation that is idiosyncratic and/or associated with literary figures. It is generally accepted that register and genre are complementary and independent. Thus, Ferguson (1983) distinguishes between the genre of sportscasts (cf. Hymes' speech event) and the language of sportscasting (register).

Different registers may be used for different parts of the genre structure. For example, in the genre of a wedding ceremony, different registers are used for the formal ring giving, for the priest's sermon, and for the songs or hymns, etc.

## 2.3 *Genre*

Genre has been used primarily by literary scholars to describe conventionalized units of discourse such as narrative, poem, play, novel, etc. Within literary theory, however, there is no consistent use of the term. As can be seen from the previous examples, narrative and poem refer to different levels of discourse. Narrative can be one subcategory of poem. Further, discourses are designated as different genres according to different criteria. Detective stories are different from historical novels because of different subject matter, while sonnets are different from ballads because of different structures. In order to clarify the categorization of genres, Fowler (1982) identified fifteen features around which genres have been organized throughout history. These features include size, external structure and occasion.

However, the term genre has not been limited to literary studies. "The concept of genre applies to all verbal behavior, in all realms of discourse" (Pratt 1981:176). Thus, conversational analysts, sociolinguists, anthropologists and discourse analysts have used the concept implicitly (see for example, Sacks et al. 1974; Labov and Fanshel 1977; Scollon and Scollon 1981). As in literary studies, the concept is accepted as universally agreed upon but rarely clearly defined. However, most use of genre in both literary and non-literary studies fits the description used by Ferguson (1986:208) who says a genre is "a unit of discourse conventionalized in a given community at a certain time, having an internal sequential structure and a set of features of form, content and use that distinguish it from others in the repertoire of the community." Scholars studying genre look for universal patterns both synchronically and diachronically.

More recently, scholars have explicitly taken this term to look beyond the genres of literary works and beyond its accepted but undefined use in sociolinguistics, anthropology and discourse analysis and have looked for recurring patterns in everyday interactions. This view (Martin 1984) sees genre as "a staged, goal oriented, purposeful activity in which speakers engage as members of our culture" (p. 9) which is the culturally defined semiotic system that realizes the register.

Such a genre is chat (Economou 1985 and Hasan personal communication). Economou has identified the characteristics of this type of discourse. It consists of the relating of events that function as a way of expressing social/cultural solidarity. Such event-relating does not have the narrative structure (identified by researchers such as Rumelhart 1975) of events arranged in temporal and causal sequence to form a story line with a complication, resolution and evaluation. Event telling and turns are shared equally among participants. Controversial topics are avoided, and when the conversation moves in the direction of possible disagreement, participants turn the conversation around. The goal is to express common cultural/social ground and avoid differences. Chat segments can occur between other segments of information exchange etc.

Other genres have been proposed by Heath (1985) who introduces the notion of recast for retelling of an incident shared by the participants and account for retelling of an unshared incident. She identifies eventcast as the description of an ongoing event while the event is in progress or projecting an event of the future. Sportscasts are the prototypical examples of eventcasts of ongoing events, while verbalized plans for specific events to take place in the future make up eventcasts of future actions. Although these genres are "a staged, goal oriented, purposeful activity in which speakers engage as members of our culture", they cut the language variation cake differently. Chat can make use of either recasts or accounts or even an eventcast as can conversation for action (Winograd and Flores 1986). In other words, genres can have other genres embedded in them. The essential feature of chat is that it is static; there is no experiential or interpersonal change resulting from the interaction. The main purpose of chat is to reinforce solidarity among the interactants. The essential feature of conversation for action (which may contain chat, accounts, eventcasts etc.), on the other hand, is that there is change resulting from the interaction (either experiential or interpersonal). There is a change in knowledge, activity, and/or interpersonal relations between speaker and hearer.

E-mail and E-message could be characterized as different genres because they are units of discourse conventionalized within the VM community and differing from each other (and from other modes) in form (explained in Chapter 3), content and use (explained in Chapter 5). However, as we saw in Chapter 5, there is no one-to-one correspondence between content or use and mode; the relationship is complex. Further, the differences in form are imposed by the mode itself and in Chapter 10 we shall see a structure (form) of function and interaction common to and intersecting all modes (which I have identified as conversation for action). I have, therefore, used the term mode rather than genre as the general term for differentiating between E-mail, E-message, face-to-face conversation and so on. The general structure conversation for action takes several forms, which do differ in form, content and use and these will be referred to as genres. Chapter 11 identifies these genres and describes one (collaborative information development) in detail. These genres can also have other genres (such as narrative) embedded in them. In Chapter 11, we will see how information can be achieved through descriptors, narratives, eventcasts etc. I will retain Ferguson's distinctions and use register to refer to particular types of language and style to refer to idiosyncratic use of different language.

### 3. Context of situation

To relate speech styles, registers or genres to context, that is, to explain ways of speaking, researchers have used the notion of context of situation, which was first introduced by the father of modern ethnography, Malinowski (1923), and later elaborated by Firth and other systemic linguists. Firth (1957) identified three components of the context of situation:
- relevant features of participants
- relevant objects
- effects of the verbal action.

Halliday, expanding on the work of Firth (1957), developed the construct register, which abstracts the context of situation by using concepts capable of relating the text both upwards to the social and semantic systems and downwards to the linguistic form. This construct is a semiotic system with three main categories: field, tenor and mode. Field refers to the process or activity within which the language is embedded and the role that language plays within that activity: "what people are doing with their world and what they are doing it to" (Martin 1984:10). Tenor refers to interpersonal relations, with three dimensions: power, affect and contact. Mode refers to both medium (and therefore distance between speaker and hearer) and the relation between language and what it is talking about. In a different but parallel emphasis, Jakobson (1960), working from Buhler's (1934) classification of three types of linguistic function, posited six basic aspects as the constitutive factors in any speech event: addresser, message, addressee, context, code and contact. There is considerable overlap among these categories and, furthermore, it is often the relationship between addresser and addressee, rather than their individual characteristics, that most affects the language of the interaction. Building on Jakobson's model, Hymes (1972) proposed eight components of a speech act under the acronym SPEAKING: situation, participants, ends, act sequence, key, instrumentalities, norms and genres. This list of categories is useful for the description of particular situations (speech events).

Other scholars have developed different taxonomies that constitute context of situation, but all agree on three broad categories of audience factors, topic factors, and setting factors. The exception is the sociolinguistic work influenced by Labov (1966), which correlates style with amount of attention paid to speech or with social group.

Still other researchers claim audience is the major factor of context of situation influencing language variation. The social-psychological accommodation model attributes style variation primarily to the effect of the addressee (for example, Giles 1980). For Bell (1984:179) language style is audience design and style shift "according to nonpersonal factors derives from audience design" (cf. Tannen's claim that characteristics of oral and written language derive from personal involvement). Traugott and Romaine (1985:28) do not take as extreme a position as Bell. They suggest that "style will always correlate to some degree with aspects of setting and participant relationship. It may also correlate with genre, channel and topic; however, it will probably never correlate exclusively with the latter, but not with setting or participants." The data reported in Chapter 5 clearly identify situations in which non-audience and sometimes non-setting factors are the major contributor to choice of mode. Les moves from the computer terminal to face-to-face conversation, and to diagrams and writing on the whiteboard, not because the topic is always associated with his addressees, as Bell claims, but because the topic is too complex to explain efficiently without interaction, checking if the addressee understands, listing and drawing. This could all be done in a completely written form, but would take much longer. Or Les moves from computer terminal to telephone because the system crashes. I could claim with Bell that in both cases Les is changing style (here mode) to accommodate his addressee, but that would oversimplify a very complex interaction between all three aspects of the context of situation.

While Jakobson, Hymes and Halliday all share concern for a comprehensive approach to language as part of communication, that is, concern for the diversity of functions, purposes or meanings such communication may serve for different groups of people, and therefore provide a useful starting point for the analysis of the data reported in this book, none of them provides sufficiently fine distinctions to describe the data reported here.

The data reported in Chapter 5 identify the three broad aspects of field, speaker/hearer, and setting as contributing to use of mode. The data further indicate categories under each of these broad aspects, providing a taxonomy of factors contributing to choice of mode. In Chapter 7, I will present the taxonomy and then explain it by showing how it represents the data.

# Chapter 7

# TAXONOMY OF MODE/MEDIA CHOICES

Chapter 5 demonstrated how Les and his colleagues move back and forth between the different media and modes available to them and choose from among them. That is not to say these choices are conscious. Rather, like other linguistic choices, these choices are part of the communicative competence of speakers within this particular speech community. The question then raised was, what attributes of the context in which the speech is used correlate with the mode? In other words, what modes co-occur with particular features of the context?

In order to answer this question, Chapter 6 presented several different models that have been proposed to explain the relation between language variation and the context in which the language is used. None of these models provides a complete description of the conventions involved in choosing a particular medium or mode or in switching back and forth between different media and/or modes. Thus, in this chapter, I will present a taxonomy of relevant context features, based on the data presented in Chapter 6.

From these data, I have developed a taxonomy that describes those aspects of the context of situation that contribute to the choice of mode and medium, a choice that sometimes results in mode/medium switching, a phenomenon similar to code switching (Gumperz 1971). As Hymes puts it:

> Cases of bilingualism ... are salient, special cases of the general phenomena of variety in code repertoire and switching among codes. No normal person, and no normal community, is limited in repertoire to a single variety or code. (1967:9)

The data reported here show that we need to include mode and medium explicitly as variables subject to choice, as well as codes, rather than only as factors in the context, where context is considered stable for the moment in question. Mode/medium switching differs from code-switching in that it seldom occurs within an utterance and it is usually linguistically marked. In the data reported here, there are no mid-utterance examples of mode/medium switching where the interactants are not both physically present; it occurs seldom, and then primarily in a shift from oral to written as when a speaker completes the utterance on a whiteboard or on note paper. The taxonomy itself could be generalizable to other linguistic choices such as register or style; however, since it describes a particular choice, more categories would probably have to be included if it were to apply beyond mode/medium switching.

The attributes can be organized around three generally agreed upon (although variously named) main categories: field of discourse, speaker/hearer, and setting. This division is, of course, a theoretical construct for discussing mode switching and mode choice. In actual discourse, as we shall see below, the choice of mode is usually the result of the interaction among attributes from more than one of these categories.

My choice of names for these three categories is motivated by a need to be as unambiguous as possible. Thus, I use field rather than topic, because it is not just the topic itself, but also the orientation to the topic that can affect mode. I also use speaker/hearer rather than audience, because it is the *relationship* between speaker and audience that affects mode: how the speaker views the audience and assumes the audience views him/her; how the speaker wants to be viewed by the audience; and how these views and attitudes have built up over time before and during the current interaction. I will use the terms speaker and hearer to indicate sender/writer/speaker and receiver/reader/hearer. I have chosen not to use the media-neutral terms sender/receiver because of their association with a particular theory of communication which is far from my enterprise here. Nor do I wish to collapse some of the differences between speaking and writing or listening and reading. I use speaker/hearer as a convenience, but one which at least carries with it the notion of participation and action.

The data further indicate categories under each of these broad aspects, providing a taxonomy of factors contributing to choice of mode. The taxonomy is presented in Figure 6, along with reference to previously cited examples that illustrate the particular category. I shall discuss each category in turn, drawing from the data presented in Chapter 5 and presenting additional data where necessary.

1. *Field of Discourse*. Several characteristics of the field of discourse contribute to mode shift: nature of the topic, organization of the topic(s), focus of the topic, and distance between language and activity.

1.1 Topic. Topic has two dimensions, both of which can be expressed as continua: sensitive/open and simple/complex. Although Tannen (1985) and Bell (1984) both ascribe most variation to audience or personal involvement, in this research environment the nature of the topic often constrains the choice of mode or medium.

– Sensitivity. Topics may be sensitive because they deal with personnel issues

Figure 6. *Taxonomy of factors contributing to choice of mode*

1. Field
   - 1.1 Topic
     - sensitive/open
     - simple/complex
   - 1.2 Organization of Topic
     - parallel threads
     - episodic threads
   - 1.3 Focus of Topic
     - on social cohesion
     - on action
     - unfocused
   - 1.4 Distance between Language and Activity
2. Speaker/Hearer
   - 2.1 Knowledge of Audience
     - who is potential audience
     - audience size
     - conversational style
   - 2.2 Role Relations
     - power: institutional, personal, and expertise
     - affect
     - contact
3. Setting
   - 3.1 Institutional Conventions
   - 3.2 Space
     - Distance between speaker and hearer
       available channels
       interactivity
       permanence
       planning
     - Availability
   - 3.3 Time
     - time zone
     - time management
     - physical constraints/touch typists

or confidential data, for example, John chose face-to-face when discussing other colleagues with Mary. People choose face-to-face or telephone conversations for extremely sensitive issues when they want to be sure the information is conveyed correctly at all levels: experiential and interpersonal. However, there are some situations where sensitive information is first conveyed through a less personal mode (a memo or electronic mail) so that the sender is not confused by personal issues. Such a choice may be made when one person is trying to convince another of something. An individual is most likely to write a well-argued, objective piece before seeing the person to be convinced face-to-face. In this case, the mode appropriate for the particular speaker/ hearer relations takes precedence over those more suited to the sensitivity of the topic. E-messages are not considered a suitable mode for sensitive issues because of the potential for lack of privacy.

– Complexity. If the topic is a quick, simple request for information, an E-message is most likely to be chosen because it is less interruptive to the recipient than the telephone and requires less effort of the sender. However, if the topic is highly complex, the sender may choose E-mail, face-to-face, telephone, or document, such as when Les went to Simon's office to reiterate and expand on what he had sent as E-messages.

1.2 Organization of Topic. Discourse topics can be organized as parallel threads, that is, interrelated multiple topics, or as episodic threads, that is, linear organization of topic. Non-interactive modes are chosen for parallel threads, whereas highly interactive modes such as face-to-face, telephone or E-message conversations are used for episodic threads. However, E-messages fall somewhere in the middle: parallel threads occur but less often than in E-mail or documents. Les, in interview, said E-messages were best suited to "one-liners". Thus, Examples 3, 16a and 16b are more typical of E-messages than lengthy exchanges such as in 15, where Les and his manager conduct a multiple E-message conversation until they get in synch and move to the telephone. In Chapter 11, I will analyze one such lengthy E-message conversation, one which has a major organizing topic with several sub-topics embedded. When parallel threads do occur in E-message conversations, they are often marked by a topic shift marker such as BTW (by the way) as in Example 13. In E-mail, parallel threads are more common as in Example 20. Peter sends this E-mail to Mary in response to her ambiguous request (using a one-line E-message) asking how to print all the files in fulist. Rather than second guess her intention, he supplies responses to both possible interpretations. Other parallel threads in E-mail and documents include dealing with several different topics in the one text.

(20) Date: 8 March 1985, 11:28:05 PST PETER at MSNVM
From: Peter Monroe
To: MARY at PARKVM
Re: Your Question about FULIST

If you want to print any of the files listed in the FULIST menu, you first must spool your printer correctly. If you are using QPRINT or something that does the spooling for you, you don't need to do any spooling. You place the cursor opposite the file you want printed and type the PRINT

command or the QPRINT command, etc.
If you want a listing of the files – i.e. a list that looks like what you see when you look at a FULIST display, you do the following:
LISTFILE fn ft fm (EXEC DATE
where fn ft fm correspond to what you would type for FULIST.
Examples: LISTFILE * * * A (EXEC DATE – gives all the files on your A-disk
LISTFILE PAPER * A (EXEC DATE – gives all files named PAPER on your A-disk

1.3 Focus of Topic. The dimensions of focus that determine choice depend on the extent to which the focus is on social cohesion or action or neither (which I call unfocused). These are not mutually exclusive in a stretch of discourse, and many discourses move from one to the other. Further, discourse intended to maintain social cohesion may be used by the recipient to initiate action. Focus and topic co-exist in any discourse. Over lunch, Les relates an episode about his failure to get Jim to install equipment for project FALCON. While the topic is "failure to get Jim to install equipment for project FALCON", the focus is on being collegial. Les does not expect any of his colleagues to do anything; indeed, none of them is in a position to be able to do anything. All these colleagues know that Jim is difficult, either through personal experience or through other stories told over lunch or coffee. When Les relates the same information to his manager, Gordon, the focus is on "requesting Gordon to use his position as manager to get Jim to install the equipment as soon as possible". However, the lunchtime chat could result in one of the hearers asking Jim's manager to install the equipment or suggesting Les use a different department for project FALCON. In such a case, the "chat" initiates action.
– Focus on social sohesion. If the major focus of the interaction is on social cohesion, face-to-face or telephone is chosen. The occurrence of language focusing on social cohesion is directly related to the potential participation in the mode of discourse. Face-to-face conversation has optimal participation potential while printed documents have minimum participation potential.
– Focus on action. E-mail and E-messages are chosen for requests for action, often in preference to face-to-face or telephone conversations. Participants do not need to spend time on social maintenance conversations and recipients can respond in their own time. E-mail and E-messages are preferred to the telephone because of the certainty of making contact. Thus, for example, Mary and Peter choose E-message and E-mail respectively so she can print out her files (see Example 20 above).
– Unfocused. There is a whole set of interactions that I would call unfocused. These include giving people information without any associated request on what they should do with the information, which has become very simple to

do with computer technology. E-mail is the mode chosen for such unfocused discourse. Thus, people find their electronic "reader" filled with E-mail that has been forwarded by a third party or that has been carbon copied. As with "chat", unfocused discourse can initiate later action.

1.4 Distance between Language and Activity. A further dimension of topic is the distance between the language and what it is talking about. Language in action (e.g. player talk in a football game) and language as reflection (e.g. a treatise on Football as an Expression of American Culture) represent the two ends of a cline, with intermediate forms such as language about an activity (e.g. discussion about how to play football). Language in action occurs primarily in the oral mode, either face-to-face or telephone whereas language as reflection occurs primarily in written accounts. Within the VM community, many language events involve participants running programs, looking for bugs, changing the program, running it again, etc. Such events include eventcasts in which one of the participants relates verbally what he and the program are doing such as the telephone conversation between Les and Mat in Chapter 3. These eventcasts fall towards the "language in action" end of the cline and occur primarily in face-to-face, telephone, or E-message conversations.

At the other end of the cline is a construction through language (for example, a paper on the theoretical principles underlying project FALCON). A document mode is most often chosen for this form of discourse.

2. *Speaker/Hearer.* Several characteristics of speaker/hearer contribute to choice of mode. The data show that communicators change mode depending on (i) whether they know who their audience is; (ii) the size of their audience; (iii) their own and their recipients' conversational style; (iv) the power or affect they wish to convey; and (v) the amount of contact they have previously had with the recipient. An aspect of the speaker/hearer relationship that does constrain mode/medium choice, but is not described in most models of the speech situation is the question of audience. Hymes, in his taxonomy, does claim at least three possible participants: addresser, addressee, and audience. This last category is especially important in any description of CmC since many users are concerned about who will receive their E-mail or accidentally see their E-messages.

2.1 Knowledge of Audience.

– Who is potential audience? Because of the ease of redistribution of E-mail, users will often switch from E-mail to face-to-face or telephone or place a "For Your Eyes Only" statement at the top of the E-mail if they do not want the information passed on.

– Audience size. The size of audience motivates choice of mode. Most communicators choose fora, documents or oral presentation for a large, often unknown, audience. E-mail, however, is preferred for an individual or a known larger audience and E-messages for a single recipient. As referred to in Chapter 5, E-mail intended for a specific audience may be distributed more widely. Therefore, many users such as Les assume that E-mail is in the public domain. Consequently, some users carefully edit their E-mail as if it were for public distribution. Les and many of his interactants, on the other hand, maintain a casual, conversational style.

– Conversational style. Just as conversational style differs across individuals (Tannen 1984), so too does choice of medium or mode. Use of mode is variable according to the conversational style of the participants. Some interactants feel uncomfortable with E-messages and never use them. Thus, a potential interactant may choose another mode to fit the style of his/her partner. Others prefer the telephone or face-to-face to any computer-mediated discourse.

2.2 Role Relations. There are three aspects of role relations that affect choice of mode: power, affect, and contact.

– Power. Within the business community (and elsewhere) power has three dimensions: institutional, expertise and personal. Institutional power refers to positions allocated to individuals by the institution, resulting in a hierarchy within the organization. Expertise refers to power resulting from a person's specialized knowledge. Personal power refers to individual personality or charisma. Interactants may choose or switch modes/media if they want to change the power relations between them and the recipient. Thus, Peter, in his conversation with Ted, moves from E-messages to telephone to lessen his institutional power as manager.

– Affect. Affect refers to the emotional tenor established between the participants and includes anger, warmth, etc. Hymes uses the category key to describe the variation in tone of voice, etc., while Halliday subsumes such variation under the category of tenor. This dimension needs to be more specifically defined so as to account for both oral and written variation. The need to use paralinguistic and non-linguistic cues that are missing in written forms constrains the use of CmC (and other written forms). This restriction on the number of communication channels plays an especially important role in people's choice of mode or medium since CmC is such a new medium and conventions for establishing voice or key are still being established, unlike other more established media (such as business letters), where genre conventions are well-established and known by the speech community. Thus, we saw Peter choose telephone as medium because he wanted to minimize his institutional power and at the same time establish a feeling of "friendliness" with Ted.

– Contact. Choice of medium or mode is dependent on the amount of contact participants have had with each other. While there is ample evidence for relationships being developed through traditional letters or on-line, if people have not had any previous contact, they will often choose a channel-rich medium to establish the initial relationship, such as when Guy asked if he could call Mary, rather than use E-mail or E-messages.

3. *Setting*. Setting includes characteristics of space and time. Space includes both the distance between speaker and hearer and availability, while time refers to time management, time zone and physical constraints. One aspect of the setting cuts across both space and time: institutional conventions, those uses of mode established as appropriate for specific institutional genres. It cuts across space and time because conventions change across time and across institutions. These changes result from recurring use for specific fields and speaker/hearer characteristics.

3.1 Institutional Conventions. While all the above choices are part of a cultural system of language use, there are culturally accepted conventions that are institutionalized. These conventions change over time as choice of mode becomes standardized among a specific community for a specific use. Hymes suggests the category norms to describe conventions of language use. For many speech events, institutionalized norms take precedence over all other constraints. Culturally accepted conventions that are institutionalized in this speech community include research reports, which are always in written form (hard copy only); presentations, which are always accompanied by foils or slides and sometimes hand outs. One convention that is changing is the move to widespread use of on-line questionnaires that are distributed and completed on-line. Currently, hard copy is also available; however, as fewer and fewer people are using this option, it is likely that questionnaires will only appear in soft copy.

3.2 Space.

– Distance between speaker and hearer. Several characteristics of the setting contribute to the distance between speaker and hearer and determine choice of mode: available channels, interactivity, permanence, and planning.

Available channels. One aspect of the distance between speaker and hearer is the number of channels of communication (visual, tactile, aural) available in the particular medium. Different media concentrate different bundles of potential channels. Face-to-face conversation can access all three channels while printed discourse does not access the aural channel and the visual channel is restricted to reader/print and does not include kinesics or other non-linguistic body cues. Similarly, the tactile channel is restricted to reader/paper and does not include speaker/hearer touch. Depending on the value placed on the different channels in different social groups, different media will be chosen for different fields, speakers/hearers, and settings. Within CmC, aural and tactile channels are unavailable or have restricted use. However, users' options may be limited because of another aspect of the context: they may choose E-messages because they are busy with other technical work. They then do not have the potential of using all the possible channels, even though this might be preferred. As a result, various conventions are developing to provide alternatives for paralinguistic and non-linguistic cues, such as the suggestion to use icons as discussed in Chapter 5.

When the content is complex and requires constant reference to system names, commands, etc., users may choose E-mail (where mixed case is the default) or documents to be sure of being clear. Similarly, users prefer hard copy when they want to use a variety of fonts that are not currently available on the terminal. This document, for example, was designed for a variety of typographical fonts. When read on-line, this channel is restricted because the various fonts are all represented by underscoring.

Because of the acceptance of silence, senders often choose the telephone or face-to-face conversation, where such a convention is absent. They can then be assured of a response, if they make contact (which is not always assured).

Interactivity. Another dimension of the distance between speaker and listener is interactivity. Interactivity refers to the potential for collaboration between the participants in an interaction. This concept includes two major issues discussed in the literature: personal involvement and cooperation.

I would argue that the aspect of mode that establishes specific options is a cline of the amount of potential collaboration by the participants. Thus, face-to-face conversation provides the potential for maximum participation by both or all participants in the conversation. Written documents such as journal articles provide less opportunity. They do, however, initiate collaboration in the form of reviews, citation, argument (both oral and written) and replies.

This aspect of collaboration results in choices of media. Some computer communicators choose E-mail to present a logical, well-argued statement in order to remove personal and emotional issues from the initial discussion. However, the motivating factor is often that in the initial piece of E-mail, the sender wants to establish a certain role relation which is best achieved in a less interactive medium. Similarly, computer communicators who choose E-messages so they can "get away with" more blunt statements may do so because they want to establish a collegial, non-hierarchical relationship which is best achieved in a highly interactive medium or because they do not want to take the trouble to adapt their language to their audience.

Permanence. A further aspect of the distance between speaker and hearer is the potential for continued referencing (permanence) which allows for multiple networks developing from the text. A permanent text can be referenced by many people and through time. Many conventions of language use result from the value the social group places on the permanence of the medium (for example, legal documents are written). Although modern Western culture values written text as permanent, other times and cultures have valued oral poetry and the telling of legends and myths as permanent cultural texts. Computer communicators make choices resulting from Western society's attitudes to permanence, such as when Les sent Brian E-mail to confirm the file names they were discussing face-to-face.

Planning. A further contribution to distance between speaker and hearer is the potential for planning available in the mode. Face-to-face conversation is the least planned and written papers the most planned. Thus, people make choices depending on which is the most appropriate for the context of situation. As referred to above, E-mail may be used so the sender has time to plan a well-reasoned argument without interruption. Further, some users suggest they use E-messages because it is unplanned and has few established conventions. Thus, computer communicators will use a medium in which planning is possible in order to distance themselves from both the content and the interactant. They then use the least planned mode, E-messages, to close the distance between their interactant and themselves.

– Availability. A further aspect of space concerns whether the potential recipient is available for a particular mode of communication.

Often people check if the intended recipient is logged on. If s/he is not, they will send E-mail. If they get a disconnect message, they may send a summons E-message "hi" to find out where the person is and how soon s/he will return. If the person is logged on, they may do one of three things: send an E-message for the person to telephone, telephone the person themselves, or send an E-message and start a conversation. These choices will depend on the field and speaker/hearer relations referred to above.

Users can also choose the "not receiving" option. When a sender sends an E-message to a user who has made this choice, s/he receives the system message NOT RECEIVING. Thus, the sender has to choose another mode which Mary did in the example cited in Chapter 5.

When a user chooses the telephone as medium but finds the recipient is not there or the line is busy, s/he may choose to send an E-message requesting a telephone call, to avoid having to make repeated attempts to connect via the telephone.

3.3 Time.

– Time zone. Because of time zone differences, people choose E-mail in preference to telephone or E-messages. They are sure of the information arriving and can be fairly sure of a quick response. Thus, Les uses E-mail to a colleague in Australia, but engages in a lengthy E-message conversation with a colleague in Sweden one evening since they are both logged on at the same

time, despite the time difference. His Swedish colleague was in fact logged on from a home terminal late at night.
– Time management. Computer users often choose E-message conversations in preference to telephone because they can do other work at the same time (parallel process). It is less interruptive. However, other people find E-message conversations also disruptive because they have to interrupt the work they are currently doing. The choice depends largely on two factors: number of terminals and the nature of the other work being done. Since Les has more than one terminal, he can converse on one while doing technical work on the other. When people are editing a document or program, they have to jump in and out of the editor to use CmC. Thus, they often choose the telephone, talking while continuing to edit. If they get "in synch", one of the participants will suggest moving to a different medium, usually the telephone.
– Physical constraints. In addition to the time factor involved in typing a long interaction, participants who are not touch typists find a lengthy interaction physically inefficient as in the dialogue between Guy and Les, which led Guy to suggest they move to the telephone.

Since language is both constrained by the context and itself defines the situation, which aspects of the context can predict choice of mode/medium, and which choices of mode/medium linguistically mark the choice? In her discussion of multilingualism among the Buang of New Guinea, Sankoff (1990) demonstrates that certain factors (namely, receiver, situation, topic, and channel) define the situation and 'predict' the choice of code (in this case, one of several languages). On the other hand, other factors (namely, tone, speaker, and message form) mark a departure from the appropriate code. She also notes that topic and tone can serve both functions.

The choice of mode and medium differs from choice of code among the Buang in that situational and topic variables are more likely to 'predict' which mode or medium is used. Some characteristics of the hearer, namely, whether the speaker knows exactly who will receive the E-message and the hearer's preferred mode/medium, do constrain the choice; however, other characteristics, namely, the role relations, are more likely to result in marked choices. For example, if both participants are logged on; the topic is non-sensitive, non-complex, and informal; and the speaker knows the hearer uses E-messages, E-message is likely to be preferred. However, as Sankoff notes, context factors are not necessarily predictive of only one code; "they served rather to define certain types of situations in which particular code choices were normally acceptable, appropriate, and even likely" (p. 37). Similarly, while E-message is most likely in the above case, telephone would also be appropriate, while a document would be most inappropriate and E-mail unlikely.

Such a situation is described in Example 17. Initially the role relations of power and affect were neutral and did not constrain the choice of medium. However, as Peter began to perceive the role relations as possibly reflecting institutional power, he chose to switch media, thereby marking the remainder of the conversation. In Example 14, John is constrained by the topic. He introduced the topic through E-messages, but moved to face-to-face interaction with Mary because the topic was sensitive, even though other aspects of field, setting, and speaker/hearer relations remained constant.

From this discussion we can see that, although mode and medium of communication are features of the context of situation, they are also determined by the complex interplay of other aspects of the context. In other words, mode and medium represent linguistic choices, choices made because of the characteristics of the particular context in which the interaction takes place. This leads to a rethinking of orality and literacy. The appearance of characteristics such as integration, personal involvement, etc. are primarily the result of the specific context of situation. When the role relation is one of high affect, high contact and low power, we would expect greater use of the characteristics Chafe has identified with personal involvement—use of personal pronouns and hedging—whether the discourse is written or oral. If the focus is on action, we would also expect more active voice and direct quotations. In other words, this claim accounts for the apparent contradiction Tannen (1985) recognized and described as *The Orality of Literature and the Literacy of Conversation*, and ascribed to focus on interpersonal involvement. As the data presented here illustrate, interpersonal involvement is but one aspect of a taxonomy of characteristics that contribute to choice of medium and/or mode. Further, the data point to a hierarchical organization of the taxonomy, an hypothesis that requires further study. For example, in the business community described here, certain aspects of the setting (e.g., time zone and availability) typically take precedence over other features in the taxonomy.

In addition, the choice of mode is itself an indicator of field, speaker/hearer, or setting through association. Thus, when one participant mode-switches, the switch is an indicator to the recipient that there is likely to be some associated change in field, speaker/hearer and/or setting. In this organic model, change in one dimension results in change in other dimensions.

Thus, any theory of literacy must account for the relationship between oral and written language and the context of situation. Recurring contexts of situation result in institutionalized choices of media for varying speech communities at various times. As Street (1984:96) says, "technology, then, is a cultural form, a social product whose shape and influence depend on prior political and ideological factors".

# PART III:

# CONVERSATION FOR ACTION

Part III examines the structure of the recurring conversations in which Les and his colleagues engage. Chapter 8 discusses the objects of previous discourse study to provide a frame for the analysis of these data. Detailed discussion of particular theories of discourse are left to Chapters 9, 10, 11, and 12 where I discuss theories relevant to the topics of each of these chapters. Chapter 9 shows how two current theories of conversation (those of conversation analysis and Winograd and Flores 1986) do not explain these data, and an alternative model is presented in Chapters 10 and 11. This model, based on the work of Winograd and Flores, explains conversation for action by describing its structure in terms of a transition network and then presenting the options available at each node in the network as system networks. The model consists of (i) the basic conversation for action network, (ii) principles for interpreting data using the model, (iii) a set of external contingencies that may intervene in the path of the conversation ((i), (ii) and (iii) being discussed in Chapter 10), (iv) a description of how different paths through the conversation for action network are taken according to differences in the context of situation, and (v) the negotiation of the conditions for conversation ((iv) and (v) being discussed in Chapter 11). The model also shows how language choices themselves help to define the relationships. Chapter 12 takes up one particular type of conversation for action, namely, collaborative information development, and shows how language is used in the joint creation of new information.

# Chapter 8

# THE OBJECT OF DISCOURSE STUDY

A close look at the actual objects of discourse study reveals that "discourse" has been used for a wide range of language activities: from monologues (Ferguson 1983) to a three-part exchange (Sinclair and Coulthard 1975) to a thanksgiving dinner (Tannen 1984); from telephone calls for help (Schegloff 1972) to a newsstory from Newsweek (van Dijk 1982); from a Nasrudin reader (Fillmore 1982) to literacy events (Heath 1983). Just as different disciplines have interpreted language variation (see Chapter 6) differently, so too have they differently interpreted the object of language study and these differences are reflected in their use of terminology.

Van Dijk (1977) uses text to refer to an abstract theoretical construct that is realized in discourse. Halliday (1978), on the other hand, says language is actualized in text. Other researchers (for example Cicourel 1975) use text for written language and discourse for spoken language. Coulthard (1977) follows this distinction but uses discourse for only one subset of oral language: conversational interaction. The ethnomethodologists, on the other hand, maintain that conversation is basic and that all other forms of discourse are variations (for example Schegloff 1972). For ethnomethodologists, conversation is a unit "characterizable in terms of overall organization (such as openings and closings) in addition to the use of conversational activities like turn-taking" (Levinson 1983:318). While there has been theoretical discussion of the use of the terms discourse and text (for example van Dijk), most researchers accept conversation as "known". In her book *Getting Computers to Talk Like You and Me*, for example, Reichman (1987) first discusses the need for a linguistic theory of discourse while using conversation, text and discourse interchangeably and without defining them, making the implicit assumption that they all describe similar phenomena, the focal point being they are all "beyond the sentence". Haslett (1987), working from a communication studies perspective, defines both communication and conversation; however, she defines conversation as a general term, while claiming that it is the successful management of *casual* (my emphasis) conversations that "enables us to interact effectively with others, and thus to grow and develop as individuals" (p. 47).

Tannen (1982) and Stubbs (1983) in their introductory remarks on terminology state they will avoid using the term conversation, which they never actually define, other than by association with the work of ethnomethodologists. This disassociation with ethnomethodology stems largely from research findings which have questioned adjacency pairs as units or turn-taking as fixed (for example, Edelsky 1981). Stubbs chooses discourse to avoid association with the European tradition while Tannen also chooses discourse but suggests two overlapping aspects which together constitute discourse: text and talk. Taking an entirely new approach, Burton (1980) breaks with this tradition by considering dialogue in drama in parallel with casual conversation.

Winograd and Flores (1986) go still further when they suggest a whole rethinking of language interactions. For them, language has three fundamental aspects: commitment, background and breakdown. Their view of commitment is based on speech act theory, that is, that an utterance creates a commitment. Further, for them, this commitment is made and understood within a shared tradition or background that includes experiential, formal and social grounding. Because recurrent patterns of conversation exist in the domain of observed conversation, these patterns become visible only when there is some kind of breakdown. Participants in successful conversations are immersed in the language activity; they are "thrown" (Heidegger 1962) within language. Thus the patterning of conversations is not present for the interactants, in the same way sentence syntactical patterns are not present for the native speaker. To illustrate this view of language activity, they provide an analysis of conversations for action, those conversations initiated to secure cooperative action. They make this choice because of its recurrence in the business community where an organization's "personnel are involved in a network of conversations. This network includes requests and promises to fulfill commitments, reports on the conditions of fulfillment of commitments, reports on external circumstances, declarations of new policies, and so on" (p. 158). They do not, however, address the question of other contexts of situation in which conversations for action recur; of other types of conversations; or of the media through which these conversations occur, which is essential for understanding the data discussed in this book. However, their basic conceptualization of conversations for action provides a basis for the model I will present here. I will expand and refine their model, based on my data.

The work of conversation analysts (for example, Atkinson 1985), Winograd and Flores (1986), and Halliday (1978) insists on the primacy of the text, unlike the work of most cognitive scientists (for example, Norman and Rumelhart 1975) and most formal grammarians (for example Chomsky 1965). Much of the work in cognitive science and formal grammar has ignored the negotiated, contextualized nature of interpretation in conversation. It is only when we focus on the text itself that we can interpret it since "the text serves as an essential departure point for analysis because the text, as it emerges during interaction, marks the relevant context of interpretation and how utterances are meant to be understood" (Haslett 1987: 143). Such text-based approaches to analyzing discourse do not interpret speakers' intentions or cognitive strategies; rather, "by looking at systematic patterns in the relationship of perception of surface cues to interpretation, we can gather strong evidence for the social basis of contextualization conventions and for the signalling of communicative goals" (Gumperz 1982: 170). In the discussion and analyses that follow, I will continue in this tradition, allowing the data (or texts) to display how participants sense what is happening in their interactions.

If we accept the view (established in Chapter 7) that there is no one-to-one correspondence between mode/medium, function and linguistic form, we also need to rethink the term conversation. In the discourse literature it is usually equated with the oral channel. However, we have seen above that conversations can use the computer terminal as medium. At first glance, the interactions built up through E-message exchange appear most like conversation. However, the data above also give a not unusual example of an interchange where Mary and Guy switched modes and media during their conversation as follows:

A1: E-mail
B1: E-mail
A2: E-message
Subsequent interaction: telephone

Thus, I would argue that conversation is not medium or mode dependent; conversations may cross many media and modes, including a face-to-face fragment, a telephone fragment, an E-mail fragment, etc. Thus, conversation is any interactive, cooperative exchange through language between two or more human beings. Conversations can be created via exchange of letters, memos, letter tapes, etc. The specific recurring type of conversation in this IBM community is conversations for action, conversations through which people make and fulfill each other's requests.

By taking the view of language as action, I step away from the cognitive science view of goal-based plans and schema (Schank and Abelson 1977).[15] Schema theory denies the "thrownness" of human interaction and its essential "interdependence of action" (Erickson and Shultz 1982), an interdependence with two dimensions: reciprocity and complimentarity. Reciprocity refers to the way participants take a previous action (including language) into account and thus an interchange is built up through reciprocal reactions. Complimentarity refers to the way participants attend to each other at the moment of communication. While this view describes face-to-face interview data, I would argue that reciprocity and complimentarity function in all conversations as I have just defined them. In rhetoric and literature, scholars refer to "audience" and "interpretation". What we have here is a cline of interactivity, with some discourse (such as face-to-face conversations) falling at the collaborative end and other discourse (such as journal articles) falling towards the other end. Face-to-face conversation has the potential for maximum immediate participation and collaboration. Journal articles are episodes of conversations in which participation is highly conventionalized. Participation can be in a review and subsequent response; through referencing in another article; through debate among colleagues. The permanence of the medium allows for ongoing networks of interaction over time rather than the immediate participation and collaborative building of a face-to-face conversation. This can still be a conversation for action. The writer's article reveals knowledge and attitudes, not just through content, but through the very language use itself. It should be made clear that action as I use it here does not refer to physical action but encompasses a broad range of activities, including the establishment of power relations or affect through language.

There are, however, stretches of discourse in which language maintains action rather than acts. There is reciprocity and complimentarity but the action language performs is to maintain itself and its users vis-à-vis each other. This is what Economou (1985) and Hasan (personal communication) call chat. We could represent the two types of discourse diagrammatically as follows:

I do not wish to set up a strict dichotomy here, but merely to draw attention to this twofold face of conversation. Conversation types do not occur in any discrete fashion; there is a constant interweaving of both types in most interactions.

From the above discussion, it will be clear that conversation encompasses most (if not all) forms of verbal human interaction. Thus, when I use the term conversation in the following arguments, I am not implying oral as opposed to written or any of the other preconceived notions in the term. As will be outlined in Chapter 10, conversation is a schematic construct. I will not use text for the actualization of language, because it does not carry with it the connotation of interaction. As I will propose in Chapter 10, interaction is essential to my view of language in use. Thus, for any instantiations of language, I will use the term discourse. Chapters 9 and 10 establish principles for the terms conversation and episode. Until these are formally established, I will continue to use conversation to refer to any interactive communication through language between two or more people. By interactive, I mean that conversation is not ritual; rather, conversation changes the shape of what is going on.

# Chapter 9

# STRUCTURE OF COMPUTER-MEDIATED CONVERSATION

In the previous chapter, I established that we need to forego any notion of conversation being mode-specific and claimed that, based on the data presented in Chapter 6, mode/medium is a choice and mode/medium-switching is a phenomenon dependent on changes in the context of situation, and choice of mode or medium itself affects the context of situation. With this view of conversation in mind, I will now turn to the structure of computer-mediated conversation. As discussed earlier, the most interactive computer-mediated conversation is via E-messages. We would then expect that the structure of such computer-mediated conversations would fit the descriptions of face-to-face conversations established by scholars working in discourse analysis. In particular, we would expect that the descriptions of face-to-face and telephone conversations identified by ethnomethodologists might be applicable here. Further, we would expect Winograd and Flores's model of the basic conversation for action to be applicable, because it describes a network of recurring conversations within the business world. We would also expect folk views of what constitutes a conversation structurally, based on the notions that conversations occur in a unit of time and over some unified space (for example, between two telephones or in a room), to apply equally to computer-mediated conversations. I could just as easily have chosen other models of discourse structure, but have made my choices because ethnomethodology is no doubt the major framework used for analyzing casual conversation, Winograd and Flores developed their model to account for just such data as I have here, namely, managers in a business environment, and all discourse theories take as given the folk-linguistic notions.

In this chapter I will demonstrate that all three models of conversation are insufficiently specified to account for the CmC data, and indeed, for many other data. Before applying the models to the data, I will describe the salient features of each model.

## 1. Various approaches

### 1.1 *Conversation analysis approach*

For ethnomethodologists, conversation is a unit "characterizable in terms of overall organization (such as openings and closings) in addition to the use of conversational activities like turn-taking" (Levinson 1983:318). In face-to-face and telephone conversations, openings include self-identification, greetings, and summons with the hearer pairing these opening moves (for example, Schegloff 1972, 1976). The ring of the telephone represents the summons in telephone conversations. Closing elements have been identified as (Schegloff and Sacks 1973):

1. closing implicative topic, e.g. making arrangements,
2. passing turn pairs (with pre-closings), e.g. "okay",
3. typing of the call, e.g. "thank you" as a response to a request that is fulfilled and
4. terminal pairs, e.g. "bye".

According to Sacks, Schegloff and Jefferson (1974), in casual conversation one party talks at a time, achieved through the following principles:

1. completion of a turn unit (e.g. sentence, clause, phrase) constitutes a potential transition to another speaker, and
2. turn allocation operates because the current speaker can
   a. select the next speaker or
   b. let another speaker self-select or
   c. continue.

These three choices are ordered as above and are recursive. In addition, there are turn-allocation techniques such as: tag questions (e.g. "You like coffee, don't you?") as exit techniques; starting first; and sets of adjacency pairs, which consist of related, ordered pairs of utterances such as question/answer or an offer from an addressor followed by acceptance in the next turn by the addressee.

### 1.2 *Winograd and Flores approach*

Winograd and Flores (1986) base their model on the five fundamental illocutionary points of Searle's (1969) speech act theory:

- representatives, which commit the speaker to the truth of the expressed proposition,
- directives, which try to get the hearer to do something,
- commissives, through which the speaker commits to some future action,

– expressives, which express a psychological state, and
– declarations, which perform the act they proclaim.
They describe the network for a basic conversation for action in Figure 7.

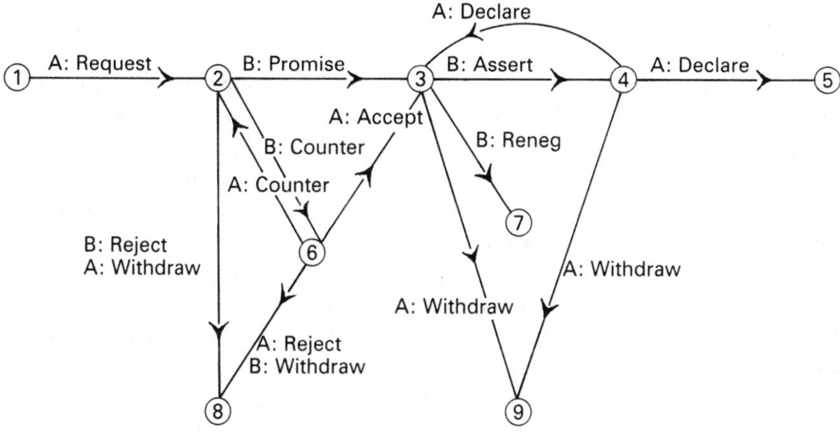


Figure 7. *The basic conversation for action* (Winograd and Flores)

In this diagram, each circle represents a possible state of the conversation, while the lines represent speech acts. The initial action is a request (a directive) from A to B. Following this request are five alternatives: the hearer can accept and promise (a commissive) to meet the request; the hearer can reject the request or make a counteroffer; the initiator can withdraw the request or modify it. B at some stage asserts (a representative) to A that the request has been fulfilled (4 in the diagram). A can then declare (a declaration) satisfaction, thus successfully completing the conversation. However, A may not consider the request met and the conversation returns to 5.

## 1.3 *Folk notions*

That conversation, especially casual conversation, is "known" and therefore not in need of definition is accepted not only in the literature on discourse, but in our day-to-day lives. In discussion with non-linguist friends and colleagues, I have uncovered some basic folk-linguistic notions of what constitutes a conversation: conversations occur in a unit of time and over some unified space (for example, between two telephones or in a room).

Having briefly represented basic characteristics of two linguistic models of conversation and folk-linguistic notions, I will now turn to examining the CmC data in the light of these models.

## 2. Applying models of discourse structure

I will now take three samples of data from E-message conversations and show how neither Sacks, Schegloff and Jefferson nor Winograd and Flores has captured some of the essential features of E-messaging. I will then show how a new model for conversation for action accounts for these data while at the same time providing a more powerful model of conversation in general. Precise definition of conversation is presented in Chapter 10. However, for consistency of terminology, I will here briefly define my use of the terms conversation and episode.[16] A conversation has to meet the formal requirements of linguistic realizations of a request for action and of an assertion or declaration that the request has been carried out. Many pieces of data both here and in other research are episodes not conversations. Episodes then are any language interactions that do not meet the formal requirements of a conversation. Conversations typically consist of several episodes occurring across time and space. Several researchers have suggested units of discourse structure. These units include local organization such as adjacency pairs and turn-taking (Sacks, Schegloff and Jefferson 1974), move and exchange (Sinclair and Coulthard 1975; Berry 1981), and floor (Edelsky 1981). More global units of organization include scripts (Schank and Abelson 1977), topics (Erickson 1982), transaction and lesson (Sinclair and Coulthard 1975), and episodes (van Dijk 1982). My use of episode as a unit does not correspond to any of these units, all of which are defined formally according to the presence of linguistic properties. Rather, an episode is a unit which a) does not meet the formal requirements of a conversation and b) is an intuitive unit by virtue of non-linguistic properties such as a continuous stretch of discourse. From this perspective, most of Sinclair and Coulthard's exchanges, consisting of initiation, response and feedback, would be conversations primarily because of the context of situation of the classroom where the interaction is formal, hierarchical and non-collaborative. As I will demonstrate below, conversations in less formal, non-hierarchical and collaborative settings consist of multiple episodes. Similarly, many of van Dijk's episodes would be conversations because he bases his notion on semantic criteria with linguistic markers signaling the start of one episode and the end of a previous one. Within my definition, topics may shift within the same episode. This view will become clearer in Chapter 10, when conversation is formally defined.

### 2.1 *First sample conversation*

The following three samples of data illustrate the problem of trying to identify the structure of conversation using any of the three models just discussed. The data come from Les and Mary's console logs. In Example 21, Brian's discourse is in mixed case because he uses a mixed-case program for sending E-messages. In Examples 22 and 23, however, Sid's discourse and John's discourse are both in upper case, the default. In all three examples, the sender's discourse is in lower case because neither Les nor Mary uses a mixed-case program and so everything is automatically converted to upper case by the system.

In Example 21, Les uses two different USERIDs on three different systems. If a user is logged on to more than one system and/or USERID at the same time, s/he may be working primarily with one, while using the other(s) for work that constantly fills the screen or for editing. If other work fills the screen, received E-messages can get lost; they roll off the screen in the middle of other text and the receiver does not see them. When editing (either a program or a document), the user does not see the message until s/he exits from the edited file. Les's USERIDs are LES and STRETTON and the three system NODES are ELMVM, PARKVM, and PARKVM1. Brian sends his first E-message at 11:14 and when he has received no reply by 14:13, he sends a second E-message, but to both a different system and USERID. He still gets no response and so sends E-message B3 to yet another system. By trying different USERIDs and systems, he might find a gap in Les's other work and so get a response.

If we try to categorize Example 21 as conversation according to the Sacks, Schegloff and Jefferson model, the Winograd and Flores model and folk views, we find the following problems:

1. Opening: there is no summons, greeting, or pairing.
2. Adjacency pairs: the initial question (B1 and 2) is answered with a question (L1). On the surface, this question does not refer grammatically to B1 and 2. It is not the second-pair part of a question/answer adjacency pair. In fact, the second-pair part of B3 is L3–4. According to Sacks, Schegloff and Jefferson, a question tag is usually used to pass a turn. In computer conversations, however, turns do not have to be allocated. Turns can be taken by any party at any time. Here, however, in B1 and B2 it is used to denote that the previous clause is old information, that is, there was relevant discourse prior to this episode.
3. Closing: B7 could be considered a typing of the initial request, but there is no terminal item such as "good bye".
4. Consecutive unit of time: B2 was actually sent before B3 but was received after. Further, this episode took place over three days. We can ask what

(21)

| TEXT | | TIME/PLACE | SITUATION |
|---|---|---|---|
| B1: | you flying directly to DC on Monday night, right? | 10/19 11:14 on ELMVM (STRETTON) | Brian sends this message to LES at ELMVM but gets no response. |
| B2: | you still flying to DC monday right? | 10/19 14:13 on PARKVM (LES) | Brian sends this before B3 but Les does not read it until he gets B3. |
| B3: | see LES USERID | 10/19 14:32 on PARKVM2 (STRETTON) | Brian sends this to LES at PARKVM2 where he has seen him logged on. |
| L1: | as it stands now, meeting on weds? | | |
| L2: | instead of tues | | |
| B4: | idiot Hess seemed to think you were there tues morning | | |
| B5: | thot that mtg from 9 to 10 would solve. | | |
| B6: | if you not in ny I'm going to have mtg changed to wedne. | 10/19 14:35 | |
| | | 10/22 08:39 | Les checks that Brian is logged on. |
| | | | Les is logged on PARKVM (STRETTON). |
| L3: | i have a 1.20 plane from sfo to dullas (sic) | on PARKVM (STRETTON) | |
| L4: | am getting into ny tuesday night & staying at holiday inn | | |
| B7: | will look for you tues nite | 10/22 08:39 on ELMVM (LES) | Brian sends this to Les on ELMVM(STRETTON). |

happened between B6 and L3. Was there interaction in another medium (such as face-to-face or telephone)?
5. Unified space: this took place over three different computer systems.
6. This sample appears to fit the model of conversation for action of Winograd and Flores if information exchange is considered action. B1–2 is a request with L3–4 the assertion. Embedded in this is another request L1–2 with B4–6 a promise. B7 could be interpreted as a declaration and so complete the conversation. However, such a characterization does not capture the intuition (and fact) that this conversation is only an episode of a larger ongoing conversation; one which began before this stretch of discourse and could continue after this stretch of discourse. When we know this, B1–2 is asking if he should change the meeting. Then, L1–2 is a request for a Wednesday meeting. Further, because it is a one-dimensional model, Winograd and Flores cannot account for B2, which is Brian claiming Les has in some way flouted the condition of comprehensibility; thus, he repeats his question. Further, their model does not take into consideration the interpersonal roles of the interactants. There is no justification (see Chapter 11) in B1 or B2 since power is equal.

### 2.2 *Second sample conversation*

In Example 22, "BERVM", "PIPVM1", and "PIPVM0" are the node names for three systems that Sid has access to.

In contrast to Example 21, Example 22 looks like "real" conversation because it has the following characteristics:
1. Opening: there is no actual greeting but there is a definite summons (S1) which is responded to with "here" (L1).
2. Adjacency pairs: there are two adjacency pairs
   - summons (S1: ARE YOU THERE?)/acceptance (L1: here)
   - request for information (S2–4)/information giving (L2)
3. Closing: there is a pre-closing item (OK), a typing of the initial request (THANK YOU) and a terminal item (BY FOR NOW) as defined by Sacks, Schegloff and Jefferson.
4. Consecutive unit of time: this all occurred within 4 minutes although one interactant was in New York State, the other in California.
5. Unified space: this took place between two terminals.
6. However, in Winograd and Flores's terms, the conversation is incomplete. L3 is a promise but there is no assertion.

There are in fact two indicators that this is an episode: the reference item "the" in S2 and a promise for action (L3) but no action.

| (22) TEXT | | SITUATION |
|---|---|---|
| S1: | ARE YOU THERE? | |
| L1: | here | |
| S2: | HOW COME THE OLD RECORD WAS WRONG FOR NODE? | Les checks directory for entry |
| S3: | HOW COME BERVM HAS ANOTHER RECORD NUMBER? | Les checks directory again. |
| S4: | I HAD UPDATED FROM PIPVM1 TO PIPVM0 ON 11/29 | |
| L2: | sounds like our data base machine is not keeping things in synch. | |
| L3: | will check with harvey | Harvey is the writer and supporter of the program |
| | | Les calls up the directory file |
| S5: | OK. THANK YOU. BYE FOR NOW. | |

1. Reference "the" in S2. The appearance of such a referent immediately makes us realize that, despite an opening, this is not a conversation but a continuation of earlier discourse. To decode "the", we need to know the following prior events and mail episodes.
   - 11/29: Sid updates his NODEID in the directory from PIPVM1 to PIPVM0.
   - 12/05: Sid sends mail to all his interactants to inform them of this change.
   - 12/12: Les updates all entries in the PIPVM0 directory.
   - 12/12: Sid is notified automatically of this update.
   - 12/12: Sid sends computer mail to Les as follows:

   I just got notice that you changed my directory entry but I don't understand how my node got changed from PIPVM0 to PIPVM1. I had fixed this sometime around 11/29. I see that you do not like to have the tie access code included so thanks for fixing that up. I note that MAX has not been updated yet. Also, how come my record number at PIPGATE, STANVM1, and MAX is 1234 but at BERVM is 5678?

   - 12/12: Les replies by computer mail as follows:

   was doing block change on pipvm0 data from the location telephone book ... since a lot of the people don't maintain their own numbers.

Sid does not receive a reply to two of his questions: 1) why wasn't his update of 11/29 effective, and 2) why are the record numbers different for different nodes. Thus, he initiates the message episode in Example 22.

2. Incompleteness. Further, it is clear that this dialogue is not complete. The initial reason for the interchange has not been met. The recipient has only indicated an attempt will be made to solve the problem. We would expect some further action on the part of at least Les for the conversation to be complete.

Thus, although it satisfies Sacks, Schegloff and Jefferson's criteria for a conversation, it does not satisfy all those of Winograd and Flores because it is incomplete. We cannot assume completion. Further, any understanding of the request in S2–4 depends on decoding of "the", that is, on knowledge shared by the participants prior to the episode we are privy to here. In particular, it depends on Sid's previous episode in which he asked Les why his own update had not been effective. He is repeating the same question but with different words. Further, their model does not account for Sid justifying his request by saying he'd done what he should have (S4). The importance of justification is discussed in Chapter 11.

## 2.3 *Third sample conversation*

In this example, Mary is logged on to the PARK system from home using a special tool called sentry for remote access. Usually users use sentry for direct access from home to the system they want to use. Mary, however, has used sentry to gain access to the MISSION system and then dialled to PARK. Thus, she is not using any of PARK's access ports. John, the data center manager from Park Lab, initiates the interaction, an interaction which intuitively looks like "real" conversation.

(23) J1: HI! YOU THERE?
M1: yes.
J2: ARE YOU USING SENTRY INTO PARK? REASON I NEED TO KNOW IS THAT . . .
J3: WE ONLY HAVE 2 WORKING PORTS.
J4: AND SOMEBODY NEEDS ONE BADLY RIGHT NOW.
M2: i'm using sentry via msnvm – does that count . . .
J5: NOPE THAT DOESNT COUNT AT ALL. THANK YOU. HAVE A NICE DAY.

This dialogue appears a unit rather than an episode and exhibits the conversational structure proposed by Sacks, Schegloff and Jefferson yet is difficult to fit into Winograd and Flores's prototype.

1. Opening: there is both greeting (J1) and summons (J1) even though only the summons is paired (M1).
2. Adjacency pairs: there are two question/answer adjacency pairs
   – question (J2: ARE YOU USING SENTRY INTO PARK?)/answer (M2: i'm using sentry via msnvm);
   – question (M2: does that count ...)/answer (J5: NOPE THAT DOESNT COUNT AT ALL).
3. Closing: there is a typing of the initial request (THANK YOU) and a terminal (HAVE A NICE DAY).
4. Consecutive unit in time: this took place in less than 3 minutes even though it was across 4 miles.
5. Unified space: this took place over two terminals only.
6. In Winograd and Flores's terms, there is an initial request (J2–4) which superficially is a request for information but is also a potential request for action. Is M2 an assert and counter to the information request and/or a refuse of the request for action? Is J5 a declaration which completes a conversation? The question here is, is this conversation for action? Is information exchange action? I will claim that it is. Further, I will show (in Chapter 11) that John justifies his request (J3 and J4) to reduce the unequal power that exists between him and Mary. Since he is her manager, he could easily just request she log off; but he wants her active and willing cooperation.

### 2.4 *Fourth sample conversation*

In Example 22, we saw a conversation that included an episode using messages, system messages and mail. Previously, I claimed that conversations can span several media and modes. How does such a media-spanning conversation fit models for conversation? Example 24 below spans three media: telephone, face-to-face and computer-mediated.

(24) Brian has just taught Mary how to use a graphics package. The graphics terminal is in a terminal room near Brian's office. Brian leaves the terminal room to see Les at the other end of the building. Mary stays in the terminal room to practice using the graphics package. She tries to use small letters but cannot determine how to do it. After trying all the methods Brian showed her, she asks two colleagues in the terminal room, but they do not know how to use the graphics package. She returns to her office because she assumes Brian is still in Les's office. Some time later, she calls Brian and explains the problem. She decided to call rather than use computer-mediated conversation because she didn't think she would be able to explain the problem clearly enough.

Brian says he'll need to see the problem and suggests they meet back at the terminal room and try to reconstruct the problem. The telephone conversation is structured as follows:

M1: (Mary makes the call.)
B1: Brian Hall
M2: Hi. It's Mary. I had a problem . . . (she explains the problem)
B2: (Brian suggests Mary didn't leave a blank between the command and the text.)
M3: (Mary reads out exactly what she typed in, including the blank.)
B3: (Brian suggests she forgot the "&" in the command.)
M4: (Mary repeats her previous statement, which included the "&".)
B4: (Brian suggests Mary show him what happened and asks her to come to the terminal room.)
M5: OK. I hope I can reproduce the problem for you. Bye.
B5: Bye.

They do this and Brian suggests why Mary's method for writing small letters didn't work and suggests a command that will do this. He returns to his office and Mary stays in the terminal room and practices writing small letters. When she has finished writing the file, she returns to her own office, from which she sends the following message to Brian:

M6: thanks very much. it worked wonderfully.

This dialogue appears a unit rather than an episode only if we consider stretches of discourse from three different media. If we do, it fits the model of Sacks, Schegloff and Jefferson and also Winograd and Flores's prototype. However, the telephone stretch also meets Sacks, Schegloff and Jefferson's criteria.

1. Opening: there is both greeting (M2) and summons (M1) even though only the summons is paired (B1).
2. Adjacency pairs: there are several question/answer adjacency pairs
   - question (M2: asking for help)/answer (B2: giving solution);
   - suggestion (B2)/rejection (M3);
   - suggestion (B3)/rejection (M4);
   - suggestion (B4)/acceptance (M5).

   There are further adjacency pairs during the face-to-face segment.
3. Closing: There are two closings, the first to the telephone segment and the second to the whole unit of conversation.
   - there is a paired terminal to the telephone segment (M5 and B5);
   - there is a typing of the initial request (M6: thanks very much).

4. Consecutive unit in time: this took place with considerable time gaps between the segments.
5. Unified space: this took place over two computer terminals, in one room and over the telephone.
6. In Winograd and Flores's terms, there is an initial request (M2) for information, Brian asserts twice (B2, B3) but each assertion is rejected (M3, M4). Then, embedded in this request is a request to meet (B4), and a promise to meet (M5). There is never any assertion or declaration linguistically realized for this request. M6 is the declaration for the request initiated by M2.

## 3. Alternative approach

How then can we capture the similarities and differences among these four stretches of discourse? While the model of conversation I propose in Chapters 10–12 was designed to account for computer-mediated conversations, it is also sufficiently powerful to account for other conversations as well.

While I will adhere to the terminology of Winograd and Flores, I will seek to make the prototypical conversation more general but the networks of elements more specific, thereby developing a multi-dimensional model. Since aspects of the context constrain conversations, it is essential that any model of conversation include aspects such as role relations that affect the realizations of various parts of the conversation. By so doing I differentiate between conversations and episodes. Conversations may be built by ongoing episodes whose structure may be very similar to those of a conversation. All discourse is dependent on knowledge shared by the participants. Episodes, however, are also dependent on the sharing of specific previous episodes as we saw in Example 22 above.

One of the difficulties in trying to apply current models of conversation is that these two models explain different phenomena. The Sacks, Schegloff and Jefferson model focuses on the exchange structure of conversation, while the Winograd and Flores model focuses on the speech act structure. Both models do recognize the other aspect of conversation. Adjacency pairs depend on the notion of speech act and its illocutionary effect, and Winograd and Flores show the ordering of exchange for each of the participants. However, these different aspects of conversational structure are not explicitly dealt with. Several theorists have suggested approaches to an integrated model without coming up with a fully explicit model which can be applied to discourse samples.

Hasan (1978) suggested both elements of text structure and their ordering as necessary for a model of discourse structure. She further suggested the importance of textual roles (speaker/hearer) and participatory roles (initiator/

respondent). Berry (1981) has taken these suggestions further and has posited a three-part model of discourse. In accounting for the structure of exchanges of information, she has proposed three layers of structure: an interpersonal layer, a textual layer, and an ideational layer. The interpersonal layer involves a primary knower and secondary knower whose contributions to the discourse are ordered, some being obligatory and others being optional. Each contribution has optional realizations. The textual layer accounts for the way turns are taken and the ideational layer accounts for the organization of propositions. In other words, the three layers refer to knower, speaker and information. In later work, she has proposed a three-layer structure for directive exchanges, with a primary actor rather than a primary knower.

Schiffrin (1985) has suggested a model with three types of structure situated in a participation framework and an information state. The structures include action (speech acts), propositions, and exchange (turns). An integrated model in these terms could be powerful, but Schiffrin has not yet explained the model in any further detail.

In Chapter 10, I will elaborate a schema for conversations and episodes that consists of a transition network describing the path of such conversations, options available at each node, and effects of context. Chapter 11 outlines the way participants negotiate the conditions for such conversations and how interpersonal relations affect choices.

## Chapter 10

# THE SCHEMA FOR A CONVERSATION FOR ACTION

For models of discourse to adequately describe the phenomenon of conversation, they need to capture not only the discourse structures but also the dynamic processes of mutually developing discourse and the interrelationships between the discourse and the context. Many current models focus on one aspect of conversation, thereby failing to demonstrate that conversation is "strategic action in context" (Haslett 1987). It is not possible here to present a complete critique of all current discourse models and the reader is directed to Haslett (1987) and McTear (1987) for comprehensive accounts of various models, Haslett from the perspective of communication studies and McTear from the perspective of artificial intelligence. I will just briefly discuss the major differences between models to develop the rationale for the model I have used to describe conversation for action.

One major difference between many models for analyzing discourse (in its broadest sense) is whether the analysis is static or dynamic, whether it is a descriptive model or a process model. The models of van Dijk and Hymes will serve to illustrate models that are more descriptive than process, more static than dynamic, while conversation analysis and that of Ventola (1983) serve to illustrate process, dynamic models. Van Dijk and Kintsch's 1983 cognitively-grounded model identifies discourse strategies such as tactics, cognitive strategies and interactional strategies, all of which are context-sensitive. Hymes's 1972 SPEAKING model, on the other hand, focuses on the immediate, contingent social context of interaction. Neither model demonstrates how the various features of the model interact, how text and context influence each other. In conversation analysis (for example, Sacks, Schegloff and Jefferson 1974), adjacency pairs reflect the dynamic processes of conversational interaction. Ventola, using a flow-diagram model, shows how interaction in service encounters proceeds over time. While this flow diagram represents the dynamic nature of interaction, it does not provide for the linguistic realizations, that is, the text actually produced by participants (see Martin 1985 for details).

The second major difference between models of analysis is the extent to which the context is explicitly addressed or is a given. Conversation analysts take casual conversation as their object of study, a standard against which all other conversations can be judged. They therefore feel justified in dealing with context as created by the text itself since aspects of the larger context (such as role relations) are static. However, even in casual conversation, asymmetrical relations that affect the interaction may well exist. Nor does van Dijk discuss the social relationships among participants. Similarly, Reichman's 1987 context-space theory, while capturing the dynamic creation of conversation, is limited to the discourse context currently relevant. She does, however, note that a discourse grammar must include scripts, semantic networks, social relations, etc.; but chooses to develop a set of independent discourse-processing rules, a choice that results in a focus on topic and how surface linguistic features signal changes in context space. Hymes's model emphasizes the immediate social context of interaction but does not show the dynamic way in which the features of the context influence each other during discourse.

A third major feature, alluded to in Chapter 8, is the extent to which discourse models give primacy to the discourse or to speaker's intentions. Conversation analysts, Haslett (1987) and Reichman (1987), to name a few, focus their analyses on the discourse "because the text, as it emerges during interaction, marks the relevant context of interpretation and how utterances are meant to be understood" (Haslett 1987: 143). Schema theory (e.g., Schank and Abelson 1977), on the other hand, identifies the plans, goals, and intentions of the speaker, while speech act theory (Searle 1969) suggests that any utterance consists of a proposition and its illocutionary force, that is, the intent or conventional force of what is said. Thus, for example, "I apologize" expresses the illocutionary force of the utterance, namely the intent to apologize (assuming the speaker meets the felicity conditions such as being sincere). Speech act theory has been criticized because of the lack of one-to-one correspondence between form and function, fuzzy boundaries between illocutionary force and perlocutionary force (the effect of the utterance, both intended and unintended), the neglect of the listener, and the possible endless list of speech acts. Most problematic are indirect speech acts, that is, speech acts whose illocutionary force is not direct, such as "Can you pass the salt?" which has the surface structure of a question, but the illocutionary force of a request. Several explanations have been put forward, including that indirect speech acts are idioms, but all have inherent problems.

Another important feature of conversation not dealt with in any current discourse models, is the paradigmatic relations Halliday (1978) incorporates in his systemic linguistics. "An awareness of what has not been said (but could) have been said provide(s) information that helps participants interpret ongoing interaction" (Haslett 1987:141).

The model presented here attempts to capture the dynamic nature of conversation, while at the same time uncovering the discourse structure and how the interaction relates to both the immediate context and the broader institutional context of IBM. This latter direction is the special focus of Chapter 12, while many of the dynamic aspects are dealt with in Chapter 11, which focuses on how participants negotiate the bases for their conversations. Further, through system networks, the model identifies the choices available at each stage of the conversation, thereby showing the knowledge participants have of what is possible as they interpret utterances. The model is data driven (including actual discourse and participants' own comments and interpretations), and although using speech act theory as a basis for linguistic options, does not imply interpretation of the speaker's intention; rather, identification of utterances comes from the communicative effect of that utterance in the conversational context (both of situation and of discourse). I will thereby follow the lead of Edmonson (1981), who suggests that illocutionary force is a function of its treatment by a hearer, that the hearer's response is central to the illocutionary force of an utterance. Further, I will not identify most speech acts as such, but use the five fundamental categories of illocutionary points proposed by Searle:

- Assertives, which commit the speaker to the truth of the expressed proposition (e.g., asserting, concluding)
- Directives, which are attempts by the speaker to get the addressee to do something (e.g., requesting, questioning)
- Commissives, which commit the speaker to some future course of action (e.g., promising, offering)
- Expressives, which express a psychological state (e.g., thanking, apologizing)
- Declaratives, which effect immediate changes in the institutional state of affairs (e.g., declaring war, christening a baby).

This taxonomy provides a useful starting point for attempting to predict accurately the functions of sentences in context, although I recognize, with Levinson "that the contextual sources that give rise to the assignment of function or purpose are of such complexity and of such interest in their own right, that little will be left to the theory of speech acts" (1983:274).

This chapter then presents the basic schema for a conversation for action, which consists of

- a model for conversation for action,
- principles for interpreting data using the model, and
- a set of external contingencies which may intervene in the path of a conversation.

Chapter 11 will expand the model by showing the relationship between context and discourse and how participants negotiate the conversation. The model identifies the components of conversation for action as negotiate open, negotiate action, and negotiate close (Figure 8), with negotiate action as the only obligatory element. Negotiate action is represented as a transition network (Figure 9) with options available at each node represented by system networks (Figures 10–13). Negotiate open and negotiate close are represented by transition networks (Figures 14 and 17 respectively). Figures 15 and 16 identify the options available for negotiate open and Figures 18 and 19 those for negotiate close.

## 1. A Model for conversation for action

As indicated in Chapters 5 through 9, conversation is neither mode nor medium specific and further, interactants may switch from one mode or medium to another during what appears to be a continuous interaction. A conversation cannot, therefore, be defined in terms of mode or medium. However, it can be defined by its discourse structure, which I have identified below as conversation for action. If conversation is not defined by face-to-face or telephone media, but by its structure, discourse not traditionally considered conversation can be classified as conversation. Modes such as lectures, journal articles, newspaper reports, and so on can be considered as nodes in the network of conversation for action identified below. Ritual such as church prayers, on the other hand, could be considered within the framework of conversation for social maintenance. I have used the term conversation because it implies collaboration and interactivity that are not necessarily implied by terms such as communication. Although the prototypical conversation is highly interactive and close to the folk notion of conversation, I will use conversation to include less typical and less interactive discourse.

As I indicated in Chapter 9, both episodes and conversations can have opening and closing sequences. These are part of the exchange structure, not part of the action structure. They contribute to the conversation or episode as an activity, not to what is happening through the conversation or episode. Thus the presence of opening and closing sequences is the default for certain contexts of situation and not for others. In some contexts of situation, maintenance of the discourse activity is as important as what (if anything) is being achieved through the discourse. In chat, the number of turns and the amount of turn time (Economou 1985) are equally distributed among participants and closing is the default. An exchange of greetings with the secretary on the way into the office in the morning is the default. When the appearance or absence of negotiate open or negotiate close is marked, it does contribute to the action of the discourse. Therefore the model for a conversation for action (Figure 8) identifies the structure of a conversation, not an episode. We will see later in the detailed networks that episodes can be identified by the absence of obligatory items. Negotiate action is the only essential item. The choice of negotiate open and negotiate close will depend on the context of situation as elaborated in Chapter 7.

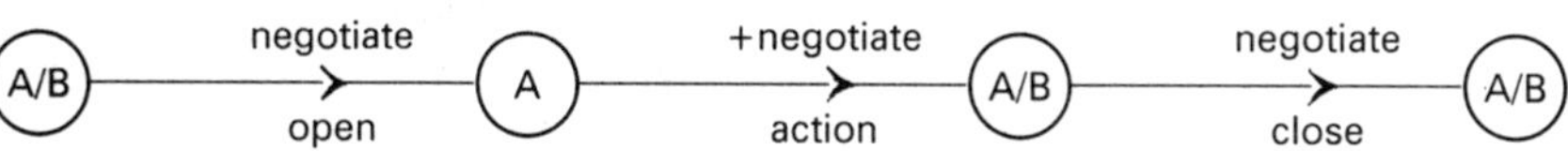


Note: + indicates obligatory element

Figure 8. *Conversation for action*

Because negotiate action is the only essential component of a conversation for action, I will begin there and move on to negotiate open and negotiate close later. Although each node in the networks below is framed by commitments made both by and to each interactant, each node also opens up a range of possibilities for future action and conversation. Both the interactional commitments and the available options will be discussed in detail later in this chapter and in Chapter 11.

### 1.1 *Negotiate action*

Negotiate action refers to the overall structure through which participants collaborate to reach some mutually agreed upon action initiated by the initial request. It must be stressed here that the mutual agreement is not static, but builds and changes during the interaction. This negotiation is discussed in detail in Chapter 11. Negotiate action is represented as a transition network with options available at each node represented by system networks. Some sections of the transition network are repeatable units and can be considered subroutines. For example, in the network for negotiate action (Figure 9), <bid refuse-action bid>[17] is the subroutine for negotiating the satisfaction of the conditions of fulfillment of the initiating action bid (discussed in Chapter 11). This subroutine may be called as many times as necessary to reach agreement on the conditions. The hearer can be satisfied that the validity conditions have been fulfilled and accept the bid. In accepting, the hearer can carry out the action requested and assert that the request has been met. The hearer can choose the action refuse option. In other words, s/he agrees that the request is

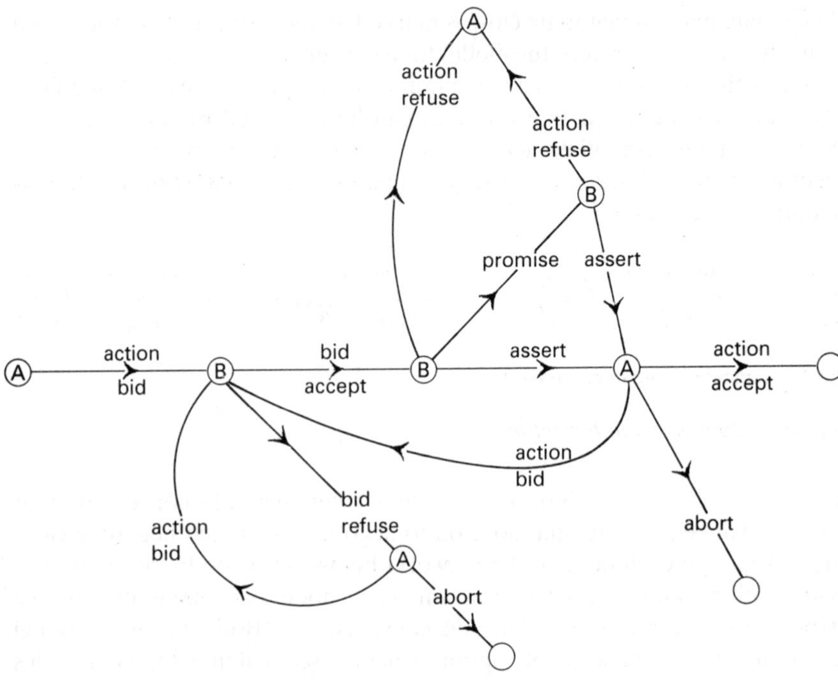


Figure 9. *Negotiate action*

comprehensible, true, sincere and right, but either cannot or will not perform it. S/he has accepted the bid, but not the action it entails. The hearer may take the third option: s/he may promise to perform the action at some later time. This option leaves the hearer with the commitment to either action refuse or action. If neither option is taken, the conversation is incomplete, that is, an episode.

The structure negotiate action identifies the negotiation for action. At each node is a network of a set of options the choice of which depends on the context of situation. It is within these networks that the negotiations for action can be identified. The options in the network are speech acts. However, speech acts can take place on different levels: interpersonal and experiential. At the interpersonal level, for example, a request by a colleague with +<institutional power> is an assert of authority/power. Further, requests can always be framed with an assert or declare, but it is the request that is salient. The networks below are at the experiential level only and need to be interpreted through networks at the interpersonal level.

1.1.1 *Action bid.* Action bid is realized by a request, which can take the form of any of the options in the request network in Figure 10.

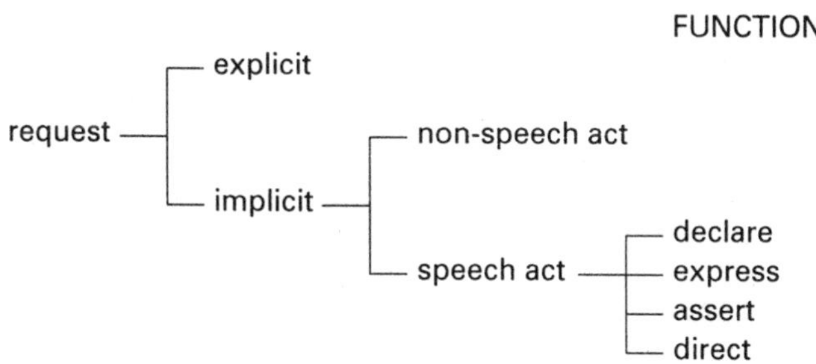


Figure 10. *Request*

Requests can be either explicit or implicit. In speech act theory, these are called indirect and direct speech acts whereas Levinson (1983) calls them pre-requests and requests. I have used the terms implicit and explicit in order not to invoke any of the arguments surrounding direct and indirect speech acts (see Levinson for a detailed critique). An explicit request is realized linguistically by an imperative as in Example 24 in which Mary has asked Les how to read in console logs and he replies by sending her the following E-message:

(24) msg mary come in here & we can get started

Implicit requests can be either nonverbal or speech acts. A nonverbal implicit request would include someone sending another person a file, implicitly requesting the requestee read it or file it appropriately. Instances of such nonverbal requests are becoming increasingly frequent because it is very simple for people to send files over the network. However, because of the amount of junk E-mail people receive, they may not be able to infer the request. In Example 25, Les has just sent Brian a file of the latest version (G) of the VM editor (XEDIT) because Brian is responsible for the editor and formatter programs at Park Lab. However, Brian sends him an E-message requesting clarification (Example 25).

(25) MSG FROM BRIANK: any particular reason you sent me XEDITG?
msg briank so latest version can be placed on public park disk
MSG FROM BRIANK: ok will do it now

An implicit request realized by a declare would include a manager firing or promoting an employee.

An implicit request realized by an expressive would include Example 26 in which Les apologizes for not having finished the report, while implicitly requesting an extension of time.

(26) Les: i haven't had time to finish the report

An implicit request realized by an assertive would include Example 27 in which Mary tells the operator that the printer (called a 6670) is broken, thereby requesting that either he repair it or he get someone else to do so.

(27) Mary: the 6670's broken

An example of an implicit request being realized by a directive is the common use of polite questions or conventional indirect speech acts as in Example 28 in which Les is trying to get essential equipment for a major project and asks Simon for a coax switch box.

(28) Les: can i get a coax switch box?

I am here using request as a general directive which can be realized by command, ask, or plea depending on context of situation (Figure 11). If, for example, a speaker/hearer network (see Figure 22 Chapter 11) realizes unequal power resulting from institutional authority with neutral affect, request is likely to be realized with a speech act command. Further, the linguistic realization of this act may be interrogative, declarative or imperative. Whether the speech act is realized directly (command with imperative) or indirectly (command with interrogative or declarative) depends on the field, speaker/hearer, and setting. Thus, in Example 24 above, Les says "come in here" to Mary using his institutional authority with neutral affect, whereas John says to her "Why don't you stop by my office?", which is a command since he is her manager; however, since he wants her willing cooperation, he chooses an implicit request with friendly affect. Further, Les is doing Mary a favor, whereas John is requesting a favor of her.

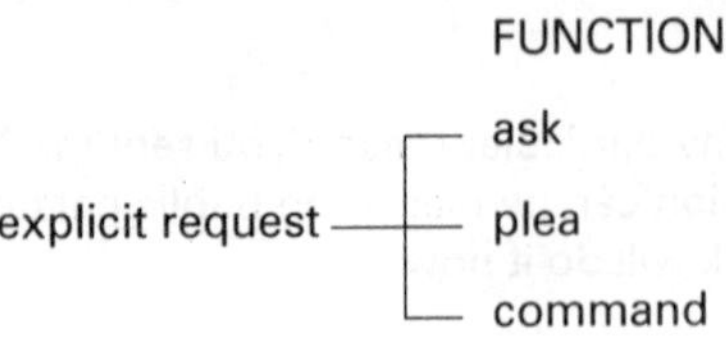


Figure 11. *Explicit request: interpersonal level*

1.1.2 *Bid accept.* If the hearer of the request chooses to accept the bid, s/he can carry out the action requested and assert that the request has been met. Or the hearer can choose to refuse the action because s/he cannot or will not perform it. Or the hearer may promise to perform the action at some later time at which s/he can either act or refuse. Bid accept is realized by an action option as in Figure 12.

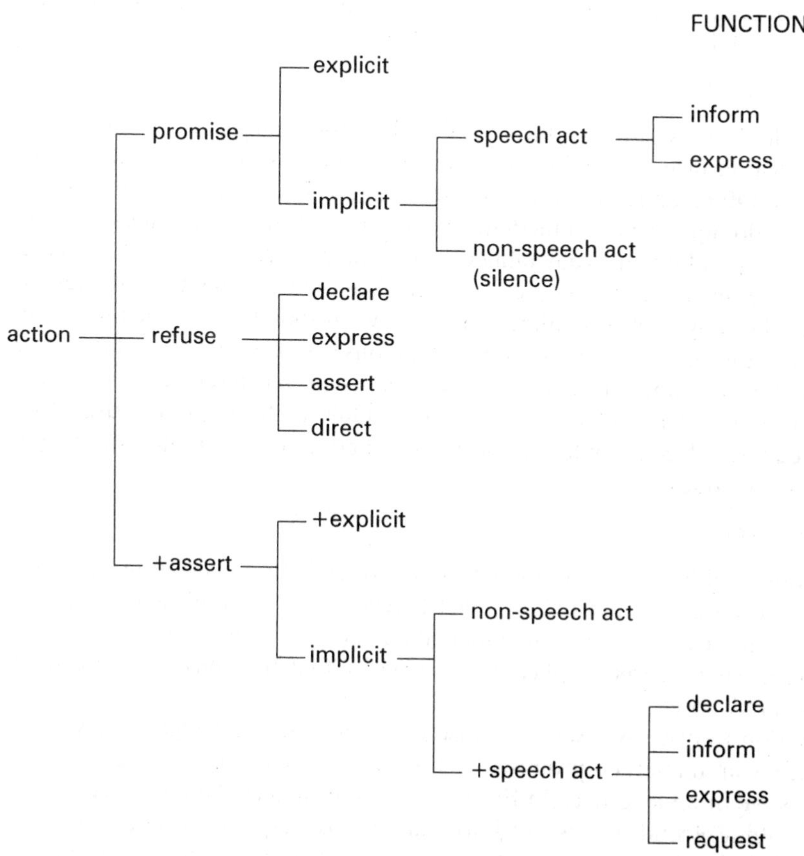


Figure 12. *Bid accept*

a. Promise. A Promise can be explicit or implicit. Example 29 illustrates an explicit promise when Les says "I'll be by later".

(29) Jim: YOU COMING IN TODAY?
Les: currently in park . . . be by later

Examples 30–32 illustrate implicit promises. In 30, Mary has been asked for a report, and replies that she'll be away until the 20th. Her manager takes this as an implicit promise that she will turn in the report when she returns.

(30) Mary: I'll be away until the 20th. Is that OK?

Example 31, on the other hand, is from someone I asked to complete a questionnaire that was part of my research for IBM. She told me she loved filling out questionnaires, which I took to be an implicit promise to fill it out, which she did.

(31) I love filling out questionnaires.

Example 32 illustrates a typical implicit promise using CmC, but one that is atypical in face-to-face or telephone conversations. For CmC, this is unmarked. Often, an E-message or E-mail request is sent to recipients who are busy, or do not have an immediate answer. In this case, requestees typically do not respond linguistically immediately. Later, when they have time, have found the answer to the request, or have been able to meet the request in some other way, such as sending a file, they will respond. Often the time delay between the original request and the response is hours or even days. The requestor does not consider this rude or unusual, but interprets the silence as a promise to try to fulfill the request. Only if the request is urgent or the requestee has a reputation for procrastination will the requestor make a follow-up request.

(32) Silence

A promise, either explicit or implicit, does not end the conversation for action since the requestee can refuse to act (because s/he couldn't find the information, for example) or can re-negotiate the conditions. It is only when the requestee asserts (implicitly or explicitly) that the conversation can be considered closed.

b. Action Refuse. An Action Refuse is typically realized linguistically since silence is an unmarked promise. Action refuse is typically a declarative, an expressive or an assertive. In Example 33, Peter makes the initial request to talk, with a second request for information. Les responds to both requests. He tells Peter the information, but instead of promising a meeting, responds to this request by negotiating the conditions through making an offer. Peter responds to the offer request with a simple declarative "no".

(33) P1: I HOPE WE CAN FIND AN OPPORTUNITY TO TALK PRIVATELY TONITE – OR SOMETIME
P2: SOON IF NOT TONITE
P3: WHEN U GOING TO CAFE?

L1: 35 minutes, you want to come over here before & talk??
P4: NO – MAYBE WE CAN FIND AN OPPORTUNITY TONITE

In Example 34, on the other hand, Les has asked Peter to meet at their regular cafe after work on Friday, but Peter responds by refusing the request using the expressive "I don't really like Le Cafe", but also renegotiates by offering somewhere different.

(34) Why not try somewhere different? I don't really like Le Cafe.

In Example 35, Les asks Ted for some information for a program he's writing and Ted asserts that "he doesn't know".

(35) L1: what is xedit/macro command to extract line from file . . . in lower case
T1: . . TO PUT INTO ANOTHER FILE?
L2: instead of 'stack'
L3: which gets line in upper case
T2: . . GEE, I DON'T KNOW
L4: i want the line into rex mixed case

The choice refuse can close the current conversation. However, it can be re-opened by the requestor repeating the original request or the requestee re-opening by choosing assert. This may be framed in an expressive such as an apology for the previous refuse. A new negotiation can be opened by the requestor changing the conditions of the request or the requestee re-negotiating the conditions and thereby making the choice assert.

c. Assert. Even though these data have many instances of requests for a file followed by the hearer sending the file with no linguistic response, I contend that the linguistic realization (either explicit or implicit) of the element assert is not optional except in some face-to-face situations. According to this model, such an interaction is not a complete conversation; it is an episode since the possibility for a linguistic response remains open.

Note that the possibility of realizing assert as request allows for cycling back because the request becomes a new instantiation of action bid, resulting in layering or levels of request/action pairs. This accounts for examples such as 21 where Brian's initial question ("you still flying to DC monday right?") was answered by a question ("as it stands now, meeting on weds?"), which was responded to with the inform ("if you not in ny I'm going to have mtg changed to wedne.").

Example 36 illustrates an explicit assert when Simon informs Mary linguistically that he has fulfilled the request. As referred to earlier, this assertive may come many minutes, hours, or even days after the original request. In this example, it was only 25 minutes.

(36) (sent as E-mail)
To: Simon
Subject: MSS
Getting error msg "VOLID 003 NOT MOUNTED". Any chance of it being up today?
Thanks,
Mary
(25 minutes later)
Simon: THE TAPE'S MOUNTED. MSS IS UP NOW.

An option that is very common is a non-linguistic realization. Unless performed face-to-face with both participants seeing the action (such as closing a door), this leaves the conversation itself dangling, since the requestee can at some later time say "Oh, I sent you the X file. Did you get it?" or the requestor might thank the requestee. Example 37 shows Les sending a DUMP file to a colleague, but with no linguistic realization.

(37) I need the DUMP package, for some CMSie[18] things. Please send ASAP.
(sent as E-mail)
Les then sends the DUMP package.

Implicit assert can also take the form of a declarative as in Example 38, in which Les indicates that it is fine to have the meeting at 12:30 in his office. In this example, there are in fact two requests, one for the time and place of the meeting and the other to attend the meeting. Les's response is then both a declarative that the time and place are suitable and an implicit promise to be at the meeting.

(38) P: OK FOR SCOTT AT 12:30 YOUR OFFICE TO TALK ABT 'SEND'
L: ok, fine 12:30 my office

Inform, another implicit assert option, can include traditional discourse types such as descriptors, narratives, accounts etc. When it realizes action, it satisfies the request by making the information ready to hand for the requestor. In Example 39 Les asks Peter for information and so his inform reply functions as an assert.

(39) L: ... where is bailey's office ?
P: HE'S ON 2ND FLOOR OF BLDG 00. EASY TO GET TO FROM PARK.

In Example 40, Les asserts that Campbell hasn't sent the SOOP module. But he also responds to Simon's implicit request to respond. Simon half-jokingly repeats his information request multiple times and then indicates snores, thereby requesting Les to respond. Les responds to this request with the expressive "sorry".

(40) S1: has Campbell sent you SOOP MODULE?
L1: please repeat, screen cleared
S2: has Campbell sent you SOOP MODULE?
S3: has Campbell sent you SOOP MODULE?
S4: has Campbell sent you SOOP MODULE?
S5: has Campbell sent you SOOP MODULE?
S6: zzzzzzzzz
L2: sorry, was in the middle of some screens, no he hasn't

An implicit assert can also take the form of a request as in Example 41, when John asks if that is all and Peter responds with a request for information.

(41) Situation: meeting

J: OK. Is that all then?
P: One more question . . about the encryption . . have you got it working?

1.1.3 *Action Accept.* Action accept is what the ethnomethodologists call "typing" and can be realized by a declare, an assert, an express, or a promise, but is not obligatory. It is part of negotiate action because it closes the conversation for action. Interactants can still have the option of negotiating the closing of their interaction through the negotiate close network (Figure 17).

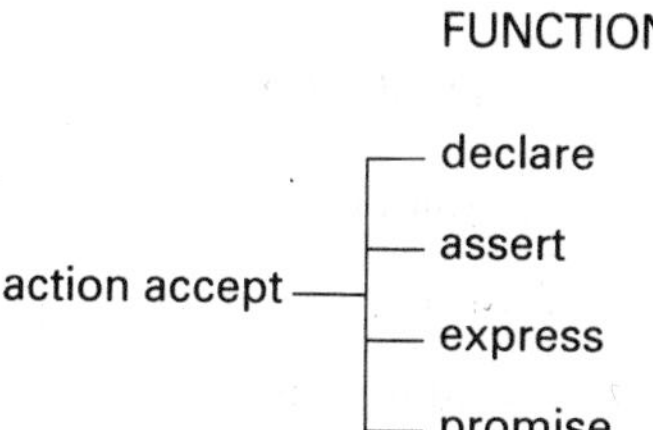


Figure 13. *Action accept*

The most common action accept is the declare option which usually takes the form of "thanks"/"thank you" (53 of the 442 dialogues end with "thanks" and one with the amusing use of "danke"). Another common action accept is the promise "see you"/"see ya"/"meecha" (10 cases) followed by a time or place to reconfirm a previous arrangement. The conversation for action may also end with an assert (e.g. "that worked fine") or an express (e.g. "great!!!"). In E-messages, action accept is usually realized by a declare ("thanks"/"thank you"), often abbreviated to "tks" or a promise.

The original requestor may not accept the action as fulfilling all the conditions of the original request, even though the requestee may believe the action completely fulfills the request. Thus, rather than declaring acceptance, the requestor may re-enter the action bid cycle by repeating the original request or by trying to re-negotiate the conditions. The requestor can also choose to abort the conversation.

### 1.2. *Negotiate Open*

As referred to above, open and close are optional and can occur in both episodes and conversations. The transition network for negotiate open is given in Figure 14.

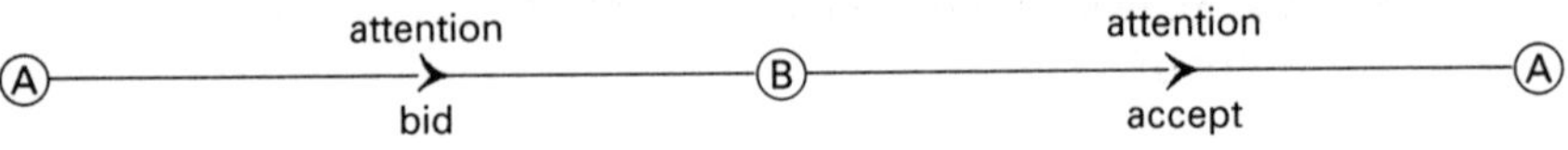


Figure 14. *Negotiate opening*

Each of these nodes is associated with a network of options (Figures 15 and 16). The choice of a path through the network depends on field, speaker/hearer, and setting.

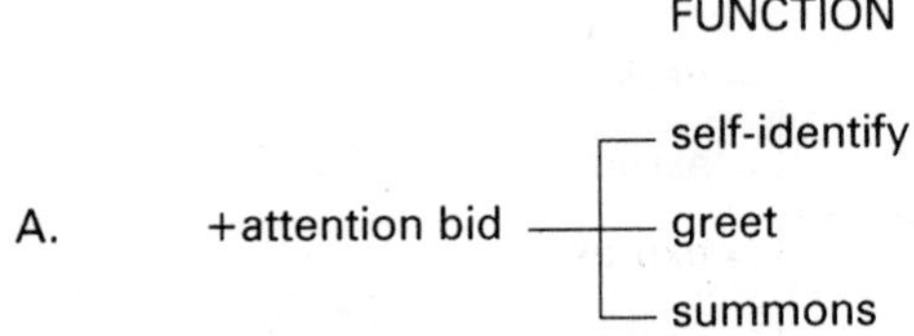


Figure 15. *Attention bid*

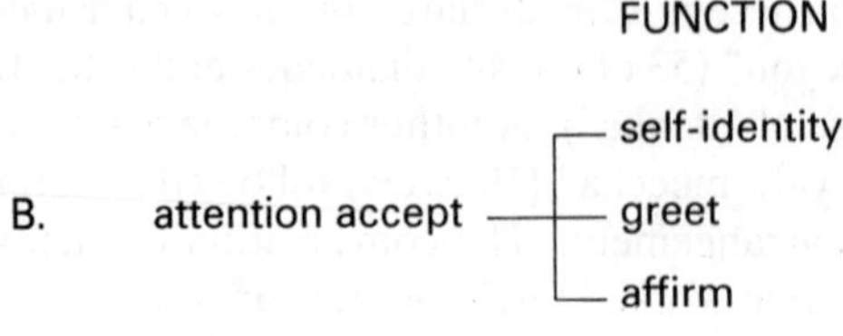


Figure 16. *Attention accept*

1.2.1 *Attention bid.*

a. Self-identify. In computer-mediated conversations, the choice of a linguistic realization of self-identify is marked. Because the system automatically provides the node and USERID of the sender, it is redundant for the sender to realize self-identify linguistically. This choice is only made when the sender is using someone else's USERID, a new USERID or one different from his/her usual USERID. In the following example, Sid was not using his usual USERID and so, when he did not get a reply to his E-message, he re-sent it, but self-identified.

(42) FROM BERVM(HAT1): ARE YOU SIGNED ON??
(received no reply)
FROM BERVM(HAT1): ARE YOU SIGNED ON – SID

In contrast, in a telephone conversation the caller is expected to self-identify. In E-mail, the name of the sender, the node, and the date are supplied by the system as in the prologue in Example 10. However, many people choose to use some form of self-identify in their E-mail. Many have developed a conventionalized abbreviation, usually the first letter of their given name. Others have included a terminal and their name as part of their automatic epilogue. For example, Stuart has the following in his epilogue:

(43) Regards,
Stuart Brandon
Park Lab
999 Computer Way
Silicon Valley, CA 99999

Peter, on the other hand, has his name, USERID, node and telephone number in the prologue and either uses no terminal or self-identify or customizes it for the particular recipient, which then functions as a closing (see discussion below).

b. Summons. As noted earlier, because of their transient nature, E-messages are often initiated by a summons to determine whether the recipient is willing and able to engage in a conversation. This usually takes the form "(are) you there?"; however, of the 442 dialogues (both episodes and conversations) in the data, only 29 begin with a summons. Of Les's 78 interactants, only 13 used a summons for the attention bid. Summons always occurs as a single E-message and in this way is different from greet.

For E-mail, the summons takes the form of the arrival of the E-mail (cf. Schegloff 1976, who identified the telephone ring as the summons for telephone calls). Because there is no question of immediate interaction or of personal/sensitive matters being exposed on the screen, there is no need for a linguistic summons to open the channels of communication as there is for E-messages.

c. Greet. Greet needs to be treated separately from summons since it co-occurs with another speech act. In E-messages, people use "hi"/"hi les"/ "hello"/"les", but include the request in the same E-message:

(44) FROM MSNVM(PETER): HI LES. TALKED TO STEVE AND HE'S GOING TO CONTACT YOU TO SET UP MTG . . .

24 E-message dialogues (of the 442) begin with a greet and only one of those does not follow with the request. It is also different from the others, combining a usual greet ("hi") with part of a usual summons ("there"). Therefore, it seems that it was intended as a summons. Of Les's 78 interactants, only 10 use greet and it is never paired by the recipient, as in face-to-face and telephone conversations (see discussion below).

1.2.2 *Attention accept*

a. Self-identify. In face-to-face conversation, self-identify is only paired in situations such as cocktail parties or business interactions where the interactants do not know each other in person. When the representatives from NEWS came to Park Lab for a meeting with John, Peter, Les, etc. (see Chapter 2), people introduced themselves to each other since none of the NEWS representatives had met any of the IBM people before, although they had spoken to John on the telephone. In service situations such as when a patient goes up to the doctor's receptionist, the patient may self-identify as the attention bid, but the receptionist does not respond by pairing. Usually, the receptionist attention accepts with a greet and affirm (such as "hi Mrs Wallace" or "right").

b. Greet. In telephone conversations, the bell ringing is the summons by the initiator and the receiver attention accepts with self-identify and/or greet ("hi"/"hello"/"John here"). In face-to-face conversation, the greet of the addresser is usually paired with a greet of the attention bid of the addressee. In E-messages, the default is for greet not to be paired. This is because, as discussed above, greet occurs in the same E-message as the request and responding to the request indicates not only attention accept, but also bid accept, without additional key strokes.

c. Affirm. In E-messages, a summons is accepted with "yes" or "yep". In E-mail, affirm is realized non-linguistically, by the recipient putting the file onto his disk (which is called "reading"). Because the realization is non-linguistic, some users have written programs which immediately send them back a response when the recipient has accessed the E-mail. However, there is no certainty that the summons was in fact accepted. It may have been rejected because the recipient may discard (using a command, DISCARD) the E-mail without having looked at it and the program still sends back a response. Therefore, this program merely informs the sender that the E-mail did arrive at its destination.

## 1.3 *Negotiate close*

The transition network for negotiate close is given in Figure 17.

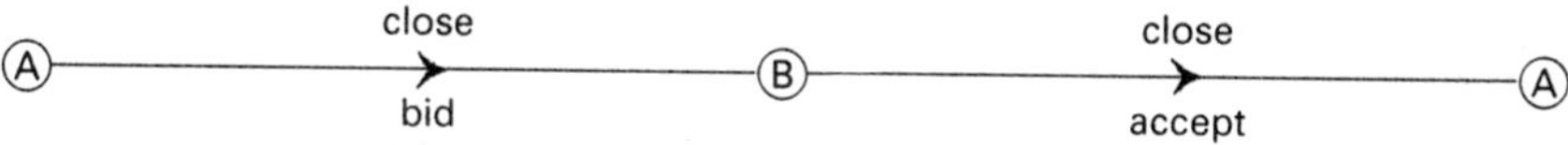


Figure 17. *Negotiate closing*

Each of these nodes is associated with a network of options (Figures 18 and 19). The choice of a path through the network depends on field, speaker/hearer, and setting.

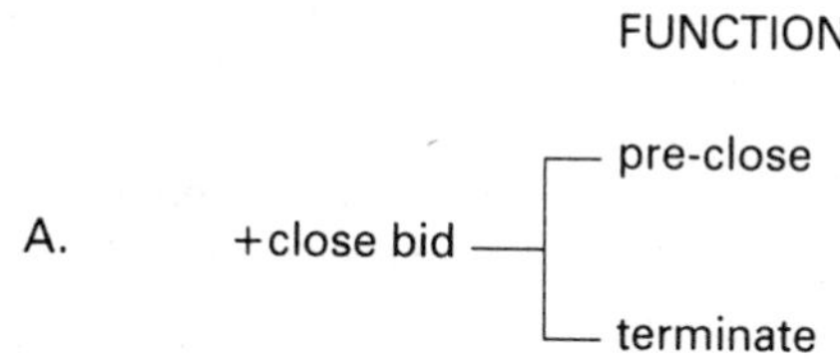


Figure 18. *Close bid*

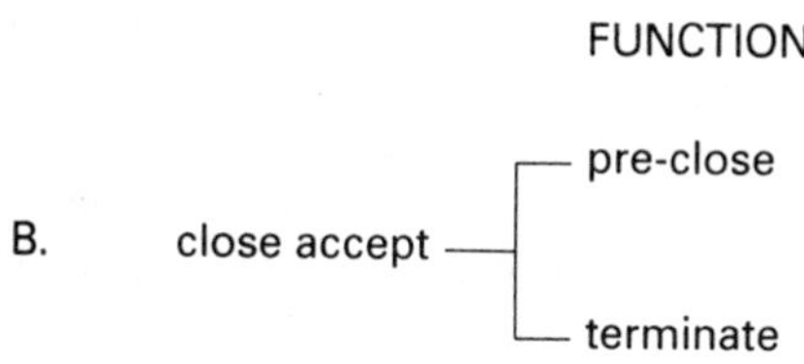


Figure 19. *Close accept*

In face-to-face conversations, closing resembles a dance. Schegloff and Sacks (1973) identified closing elements as:

1. closing implicative topic, e.g. making arrangements,

2. passing turn pairs (with pre-closings), e.g. “okay”,
3. typing of the call, e.g. “thank you” as a response to a request that is fulfilled, and
4. terminal pairs, e.g. “bye”.

Of the 442 E-message dialogues, only 63 have any closing element; E-message conversations are often suspended without any formal linguistic realization of the closing. Silence (that is, the absence of any further E-messages) may indicate a closing of the conversation. Although ambiguous, this silence does not violate Grice’s maxims of conversation (1975) since it is not considered rude by CmC communicators who know that systems can fail, E-messages can roll off the screen, and, most importantly, that face-to-face and/or telephone interruptions to CmC conversations take precedence.

1.3.1 *Close bid.* As I have already indicated, interactants may close the interaction as well as the conversation for action. Of the 63 action accepts in the dialogue data, 14 were preceded by the pre-close “ok”, and only 7 with terminal items. Terminal items (with frequency) are “I gotta(gonna) go/I’ve go to go” (5), “time to go” (1), and “bye” (1). Only two E-message dialogues close with a pre-close, a typing and a terminal, unlike face-to-face and telephone conversations in which all three are likely to occur. Just as silence can be interpreted as a suspension of the conversation, so too recipients accept the presence of any closing element as an almost non-negotiable indication of the closing of the conversation.

As indicated above in the discussion on openings, senders of E-mail will sometimes include a terminal item (usually “regards”) or a typing (usually “thanks”), which Mary does in Example 36 when she typed the conversation by using “thanks” and then self-identified with “Mary”. It’s as though the name impersonally supplied by the computer does not carry the same value as the personal signing by the individual, a strategy similar to that used in typewriting—although we may type our name at the end of a letter, we also sign it by hand. Many have developed a conventionalized abbreviation, usually the first letter of their given name while others include a terminal and their name as part of their automatic epilogue. Users can design their own epilogues, that is, some information that is automatically appended to the end of E-mail by the computer system and that they do not have to type every time as discussed above.

1.3.2 *Close Accept.* Also there is no pairing of pre-close or terminate in the E-message data, unlike face-to-face and telephone conversations where pairing is unmarked. Thus, for example, “I gotta go” successfully ended a conversation without any further closing items from either party. Face-to-face and telephone conversations, on the other hand, often include negotiations that re-open, or, as Schegloff and Sacks (1973) claim, "opening up closings".

Close accept has been included in the model to account for its occurrence in face-to-face and telephone data.

Although it will not be discussed in detail, it is worth mentioning here that turn-taking, the local management of conversations discussed by conversation analysts also has different norms in CmC conversations than in face-to-face or telephone conversations.

Because of the nature of the medium, the feature "one party talks at a time" is not preserved: the sender may make a second move before receiving a response to the first and a message may interrupt a turn. Further, turn-allocation techniques such as adjacency pairs or tag questions are largely absent. This complex interaction results in layered topics, multiple speech acts and interleaved turns. These characteristics have been described in detail elsewhere (Murray 1989). Thus, I will provide one example here to give the flavor of turn-taking in E-message conversations. Example 45 illustrates how an E-message may interrupt a turn or even a move. The sender may continue with the move or, as a result of the message, abort the move or change it. In Example 45, Peter's message (P1) interrupts Ted's turn of listing systems where 'it' is operating. Then Peter's message (P2) arrives before Ted has replied to P1. As a result, Ted's last utterance consists of two moves: responses to two of Peter's utterances (P1 and P2).

(45) T1: THEY HAVE IT RUNNING DOWN AT THE LAB (ON SYS21)
P1: yeah – using lab 'f' for home terminal support i bet!
T1: ALSO ON SYS24. ISN'T IT SOMETHING?
P2: what would be the effect of having the home term with ymon using a high speed modem?
T2: ALEX WAS INTERESTED IN PUTTING IT UP ON SYS54
(response to P1)
HIGH SPEED WOULD MAKE IT REALLY LOOK SWEET.
(response to P2)

E-mail conversations, like regular mail, may also contain overlapping (or crossed) turns, and second moves before a response is received to the first move. Since E-mail is relatively easy, overlapping and multiple moves before responses are common. In regular mail, writers usually check their letters thoroughly to ensure they have not omitted anything. In E-mail, it is common for a second E-mail to be sent on the heels of the first, with a metalinguistic comment, for example, "forgot to say", "BTW", or even the use of "..." in E-messages.

In this chapter, I have only discussed the networks for the basic conversation for action. It must be borne in mind, that all the networks presented are options available along with other network options. For example, for conversations for action to be successfully completed, participants need to cooperate. This cooperation depends on one aspect of the context of situation, interpersonal relations and will be discussed in Chapter 11.

## 2. Interpretive principles

For any linguistic event, there are at least three interpretations: the speaker's, the hearer's and the eavesdropper's (or analyst), none of which is privileged; each is valid as a representation of the interaction. As analysts, the most we can do is use triangulation and/or apply consistent principles for our own interpretations, principles that I will now outline.

Only request and assert are obligatory for a conversation to be complete. What separates episodes from conversations is that episodes have either no assert element or the request element is a reformulation of a former request or both. However, analysts need to make some pragmatic operational decisions when determining whether stretches of discourse are episodes or conversations. For contexts of situation in which the action (not just the conversation) takes place with −<face-to-face>, the following operational requirements hold. The absence of a linguistic realization of assert means only that the conversation may be incomplete, not that there was failure to secure cooperative action. That is, silence must be interpreted as dynamic but ambiguous. If linguistic evidence for action is missing, the analyst can only assume incompleteness. If assert is realized non-linguistically, the option to realize it linguistically is always open. Brian (Example 37 in Chapter 10) requests a file from Les and Les sends it to him, but Les does not indicate this linguistically nor does Brian declare with "thanks". Several days later, Brian and Les have lunch together and Les asks "did you get the script file?" By using this implicit speech act of a request for information, Les asserts he has sent the file, thereby responding to Brian's initial request.

Similarly, for episodes tied back to previous episodes, if there is no linguistic evidence (in the form of reference, etc. or existence of the actual episode), the analyst has to assume completeness. For situations where the action takes place with +<face-to-face>, analysts can only assume the conversation is complete if they are certain both requestor and requestee know the action has been carried out. Even with ethnographic studies, it is not possible to collect all the episodes of a conversation and so the analyst must make interpretive decisions when the data do not provide sufficient evidence.

In Example 21 above, if Brian had asked "When are you flying to DC?" and there was no evidence of other preceding episodes, this stretch could be called a conversation even though it does depend on Brian's knowledge that Les was flying to DC. The use of a "when" question does not reinforce any previous contact whereas in the actual example the use of "still" and "right" does. The "when" question asks for new information rather than confirmation of shared information.

## 3. External contingencies

In addition to the above formal model and interpretive principles, it is necessary to posit a set of external contingencies which, for obvious reasons, I call deus ex machina:

1. other person/information resolution
2. initial need no longer a need
3. partial solution resulting in change of need
4. no new information to hand
5. interruption of interaction

Since commitment lies with both requestor and requestee, if there is no commitment, a breakdown occurs in the conversation. We saw above in Example 22, that the conversation was incomplete because Les made a promise but no action. If Les subsequently found the answers to Sid's information requests and asserted these to Sid, the conversation would be complete and there would be no breakdown. If, however, Les did and said nothing further, there would be breakdown. Further, if Sid found answers to his requests either from another person or through his own attempts at resolving the problem, there would be breakdown unless he informed Les of the resolution. Commitment lies with both initiator and responder. Thus, if external contingency 1 occurs, the responder needs to be released from his/her commitment to action. If Sid does not release Les from the commitment, the conversation is "hung". Similarly, the occurrence of external contingency 2 or 3 requires Sid to release Les from his/her commitment or re-formulate the initial request.

The occurrence of 4 or 5 also results in the initial conversation and the action getting "hung". Completion depends on some new intervention to become "unhung". For external contingency 4, this usually involves a move away from the initial negotiation/action until new information is at hand. This may involve participation in another conversation for action. If the interaction is interrupted (for example, by a telephone call, by a system going down) the move away from the initial negotiation will be unrelated to the interrupted conversation. For the conversation to reach resolution, one of the participants needs to re-enter the negotiation. This re-entry may occur hours or even days after the initial action bid.

This set of external contingencies explains the initiation and "hung" status of episodes, those dynamic, ongoing stretches of discourse which combine into conversations for action.

This description of conversations and episodes claims that participants in conversations have a schema for conversations for action in which bid for action and action are obligatory. Thus, the absence of the element action leaves participants with an incompleteness and the possibility of the conversation being taken up again later. This accounts for episodes and moves away from the initial action bid that result from deus ex machina. Participants do not consider such moves or episodes unexpected or strange; they are contributions to the final resolution through action. Further, the above principles for defining a conversation allow the discourse analyst to make consistent decisions concerning the status of discourse stretches and so make comparisons across media, across modes, and across different role relations and fields.

The model with its interpretive principles is important not only for discourse analysts, but also for computer (and other) communicators. Managers need to know what requests made by them and to them are still outstanding. They need to know what promises they have made and have been made to them. In other words, they need to know which of their interactions are episodes and which are conversations. This model of conversation applies to a broad range of human interaction through language. It allows us to view scholarly discourse and other modes from a new perspective: modes such as lectures and journal articles are part of ongoing conversations for action. Such texts, therefore, might be requests for action or asserts through informs, expressives, etc.

In Chapter 11, I will expand the model, identifying how interpersonal relations affect the choices made, and showing how interactants negotiate the conditions for their conversations.

# Chapter 11

# NEGOTIATING THE CONDITIONS FOR CONVERSATION[19]

In Chapter 10 we saw that the subroutine <bid refuse-action bid> was a repeatable unit, available at any node in the negotiate action network. In this chapter I will discuss this subroutine, showing how a hearer can refuse a bid for conversation by questioning the validity conditions of the speaker's utterance. I will explain the subroutine below for the case where it is invoked after the initial action bid. At other nodes, some of the specifics would differ, but the general principles hold.

## 1. Bid refuse: Negotiating conditions of agreement

### 1.1. *Requestee refusal*

In the negotiate action network, bid refuse is realized by a request to renegotiate the validity conditions (see Figure 20) of the initiating speech act. This should not be confused with a refusal to comply with the initial request by not acting. When a requestee refuses the bid s/he questions the validity of the request, but does not necessarily refuse to comply with the request. In other words, the requestee responds to the implicatures, not the illocutionary force of the request by questioning whether the requestor is actually abiding by the cooperative principle or not.

Grice's four maxims of conversation (quality, quantity, relevance, and manner) do not include a principle that is often invoked in my data, namely, appropriateness to the interpersonal relations of the interactants. Habermas (1979), on the other hand, collapses Grice's maxims of relevance and manner under comprehensibility, and introduces the condition of rightness to account for interpersonal relations. For these data, therefore, I will use Habermas's four validity conditions that operate to ground speech acts (see Figure 20). The speech act must be comprehensible so both speaker and hearer can understand each other. The speaker must utter a propositionally true utterance so the hearer can share the speaker's knowledge. The speaker must express his utterance sincerely for the hearer to trust him. Finally the speaker must express the utterance from a position of rightness (appropriate to their interpersonal relations) that the hearer shares. These validity claims may be negotiated at any node in the network. The hearer refuses to accept the bid for action by requiring justification of one or more of the validity claims. To do this, the hearer may make an offer, request a repeat or request a clarification (see Figure 20).

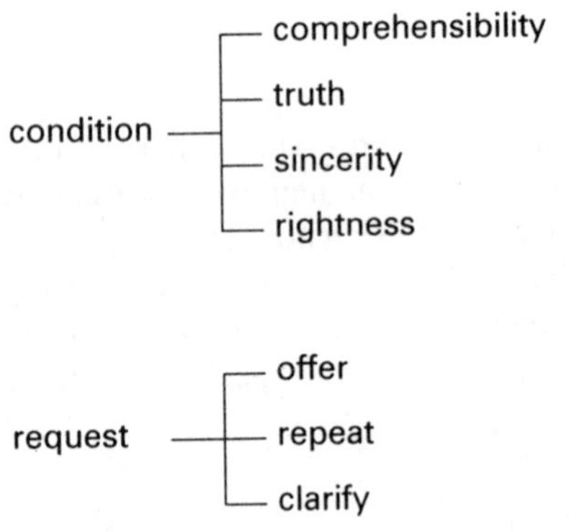


Figure 20. *Validity Conditions*

1.1.1 *Comprehensibility*. In Example 46, Simon has sent an E-message to Les; but, because Les is in the middle of executing some technical work, his screen rolls forward before he has a chance to read Simon's message. As the screen rolls, he only notices that there is an E-message from Simon; so, he asks Simon to repeat the E-message. In other words, Simon's E-message did not fulfill the condition of comprehensibility. Other examples include not hearing someone in a face-to-face conversation, or the use of language the requestee does not understand.

(46) Les: please repeat, screen cleared

1.1.2 *Truth*. The condition of truth is often questioned by the hearer because s/he cannot match the proposition(s) of the utterance with his/her own knowledge of the world. In Example 47, Mary is logged on to the PARK system from home using a special tool called sentry for remote access. Usually users use sentry for direct access from home to the system they want to use. Mary, however, has used sentry to gain access to the MISSION system and then dialled across an internal network to PARK. Thus, she is not using any of PARK's access ports. John, the data center manager from Park Lab asks Mary if she is using SENTRY into PARK, framing his request in an inform in which he tells her why he wants this information. However, Mary is not sure whether her state of affairs (using SENTRY via MSNVM) meets the conditions of John's request; she doesn't know whether she is in fact using one of the only two available ports. To her, John's request does not meet the validity condition of truth. Therefore she makes a request for clarification by stating how she is logged on to PARK and asking if that is what John means.

(47) J1: ARE YOU USING SENTRY INTO PARK? REASON I NEED TO KNOW IS THAT . .
J2: WE ONLY HAVE 2 WORKING PORTS.
J3: AND SOMEBODY NEEDS ONE BADLY RIGHT NOW.
M1: i'm using sentry via msnvm – does that count . . .
J4: NOPE THAT DOESNT COUNT AT ALL. THANK YOU. HAVE A NICE DAY.

1.1.3 *Sincerity.* Habermas's third validity claim, sincerity, states that the speaker must express his utterance sincerely so the hearer will trust him. This is similar to Grice's maxim of quality. Because questioning another's sincerity is dispreferred, there are few examples in these data; instead, requestors themselves justify the sincerity of their requests (discussed below under "Justification"). The few examples that do occur in these data are directed at a third person, not at the addressee, as in Example 48. Les has asked Ted, a system programmer, whether he is running any projects on another lab's mainframe. Ted responds by stating that the machine is "down", and hence he cannot work on that machine. The operators and system analysts at that site have promised the machine will be "up" soon, but he questions their sincerity by telling Les "I don't believe it".

(48) Ted1: . . . Currently, the thing is down (Hardware problem)
Ted2: . . . They say it'll be up at 4, but I don't believe it.

1.1.4 *Rightness.* The fourth validity claim that can be negotiated is that the utterance needs to be made so that it is appropriate to the interpersonal relations between the speaker and hearer. When asked to respond to a questionnaire that I sent out to users of E-mail and E-message, one of the subjects called me to say that he would respond when he had management approval to do so. This subject (and others) questioned my legitimacy to do such a questionnaire without going through their management chain. In other words, they did not know whether the institutional relationships between me and them included the filling out of a questionnaire.

### 1.2 *Requestor response*

Once the requestee has questioned the validity claim(s), the requestor can justify the claim and/or reformulate the initial action bid, deny the claim and repeat the original action bid, or abort the bid because it is no longer relevant. In Example 46, Simon sends his E-message to Les again, thereby agreeing with Les's claim that his request was not comprehensible. In Example 49, Les questions the truth of Peter's suggestion that they talk privately at the cafe because he knows from past experience that it is unlikely they will have any private time. He questions the truth claim by making an offer; however, Peter denies the truth claim by rejecting Les's offer and merely repeats his original request.

(49) P1: I HOPE WE CAN FIND AN OPPORTUNITY TO TALK PRIVATELY TONITE – OR SOMETIME
P2: SOON IF NOT TONITE
P3: WHEN U GOING TO CAFE?
L1: 35 minutes, you want to come over her before & talk??
P4: NO – MAYBE WE CAN FIND AN OPPORTUNITY TONITE

In Example 47, John aborted his request after Mary questioned the truth of his implicit request. He said "nope. that doesn't count at all" because he could no longer request that Mary relinquish her port since the one she was using was not on his system.

This subroutine <bid refuse-action bid> may be called as many times as necessary to reach agreement on the conditions. The hearer signals that the conditions have been met by a bid accept. This may take the form of an action that fulfills the initial bid, an action refuse that accepts the bid as legitimate but indicates an inability to act, or a promise that commits the promiser to either action or action refuse in order to complete the conversation. At any node in the network, the subroutine <bid refuse-action bid> may be called to renegotiate the conditions.

### 1.3 *Justification: Pre-establishing the conditions*

Since any action bid can potentially be refused, and refusal is dispreferred, requestors often attempt to forestall refusal and negotiation of the validity claims by justifying their request. Justification can be expressed by explicitly stating one or more of the four validity claims. The choice of different options of justification is dependent on the interpersonal relations (in particular, power) of the participants. Therefore, before giving examples of justification of all four validity claims, I will discuss interpersonal relations and present an interpersonal network of power.

Different researchers have identified different dimensions of social interaction that are relevant to interpersonal linguistic choices. These include power and solidarity (Brown and Gilman 1960); formality and informality (Ellis and Ure 1969); and power, contact, and affect (Martin unpublished manuscript). Of particular relevance in the work setting is the interpersonal dimension of power. Although the institution may assign certain power roles, individuals may choose to downplay or even reverse unequal power relations, achieving such changes in power relations through choices within linguistic systems. One such system is justification.

For conversations for action to be successfully completed, participants need to cooperate. This cooperation can be achieved through any of the paths through the power network (see Figure 21). The network includes two parallel choices, equality of power and source of power, options being chosen from both.

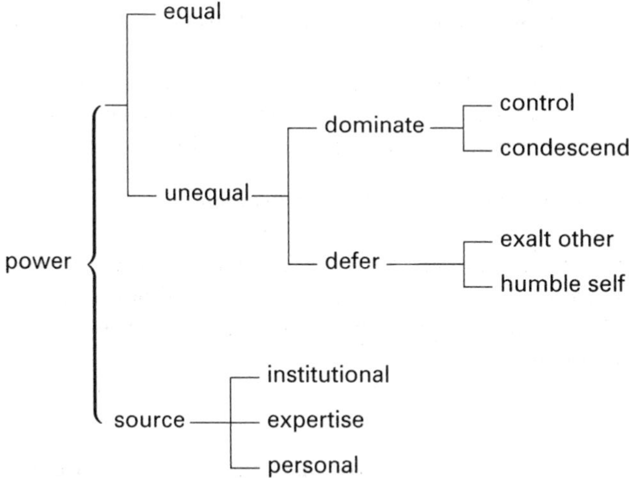


Figure 21. *Power network*

When power is unequal and the requestor chooses to use his/her institutional position of power to ensure cooperation, the option dominate is chosen and the requestor does not justify the request, e.g. "Finish the report by 3 o'clock"). When the power is unequal, but the requestor chooses to defer to the interactant with less power, s/he will justify the request. When power is equal, the requestor may choose to use justification to secure the recipient's cooperation. The use of justification varies across users, from those who rarely use it to those who always do, which in itself is a statement of the power relations between the participants.

In Example 47, when John asked Mary whether she was using SENTRY into PARK, he framed his request with a justification for his question and potential request for Mary to relinquish her use of the port. John could have used his institutional power to ask Mary to log off. Instead, he justifies his question and tells her of a "need" in order to secure her cooperation. This allows her to take the responsibility for logging off. In this situation, however, she was not using one of PARK's ports and so was in no position to volunteer help.

Depending on which outcome from the power network people wish to achieve, they will choose different options from the justification network to establish the validity claim of their request: its comprehensibility, truth, sincerity, and/or rightness. Thus, in order to secure cooperation, requestors use different options from the justification network in order to change interpersonal relations. They shift responsibility and thereby change equal power to deference to the recipient or change their position of dominance to one of deference. This power shift gives the recipient freedom to cooperate.

1.3.1 *Comprehensibility.* In Example 50, when Mary wants to make a request of Peter, but is not sure whether she knows how to express it comprehensibly, but wants to ensure a response, she justifies the possible lack of comprehensibility.

(50) Mary: i don't know if this makes sense, but . . .

1.3.2 *Truth.* The validity claim that is most frequently established by the requestor is truth. Depending on the interpersonal network option the requestor chooses, different options may be chosen from the justification of truth network (see Figure 22).

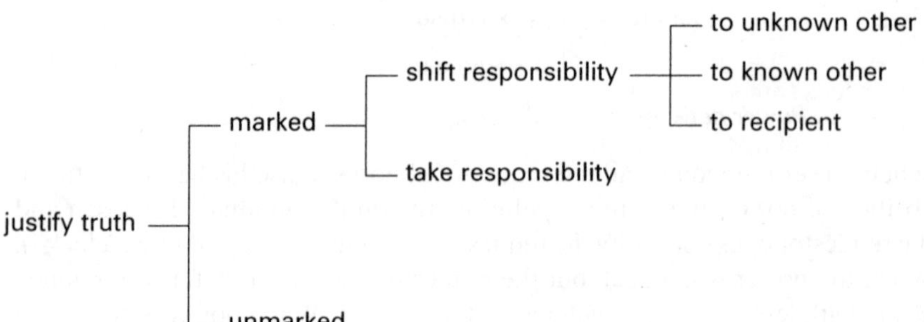


Figure 22. *Justification of truth network*

Unmarked justification is used when power is equal and the requestor does not wish to change relative status. It is realized by representatives (Searle 1976), indicative mood and absence of modals as in Example 51. Marked justification, on the other hand, is often realized by expressives, interrogatives, modals and "need" statements (see Examples 55 and 58).

Les has sent Peter two files, one a soft copy of a paper formatted for printing, the other, foils formatted for printing on a special printer that does large fonts for foils. Peter does not have this special printer and/or the software that supports it. Thus, when he tries to print the files in hard copy, his system sends back messages that it cannot recognize the formatting commands (tags) Les has put in the files. Peter requests Les to send him what is necessary to format the files so they are readable on his printer (a 6670). However, he frames his request with an inform which justifies the truth of the request.

(51) From: Peter Munroe PETER at MSNVM
To: STRETTON at PARKVM
I just tried to script the two files you sent on SEND performance. The S63PAP SCRIPT file was OK except for the " :lineref" tag. Our version of Script[20] doesn't recognize that tag.
The other file, S63FOIL SCRIPT didn't get off the ground. We don't know of any program that recognizes the commands that are in S63FOIL.
Could you send me a formatted version that I could print on our 6670?

Justification is marked by shifting responsibility to others or by the speaker taking the responsibility. Taking responsibility is realized by the verb "want". When Les says "i want ..." (Example 52) to Ted, Ted is unlikely to negotiate the validity claim of the truth of the request. One cannot deny another's "wants", only their "needs".

(52) Les: i want the line into rex in mixed case

When Les shifts the responsibility to an unknown other as in Example 53, the recipient can query the validity claim. We can question whether someone really needs something, but not whether they want it.

(53) Les: (i) need a new system disk

Similarly, responsibility can be shifted by using "it's necessary" or passives. Requestors seldom take responsibility because it closes negotiation of validity claims and forces the recipient to cooperate. Rather, requestors choose to justify their requests by shifting the responsibility for their requests to some "other". The responsibility can be shifted to the recipient by taking the implicit speech act path through the action bid network. When someone sends Les the

E-messages in Example 54, without an explicit request, the responsibility for both request and action moves to the recipient.

(54) I DON'T HAVE A 370 PRINC. OF OPS.

1.3.3 *Sincerity.* The third claim, sincerity, is more often justified by the speaker than questioned by the recipient. When Al wants to know how to link to one of Les's disks, he establishes sincerity by prefacing the request in Example 55.

(55) Al: I know this will sound silly but . . . How do I link to stretton 192 and specify the password??

He justifies his sincerity because he assumes he should know how to "link" and Les will either not respond or will himself ascribe "silliness" to Al. Al therefore preempts such a situation by humbling himself (see interpersonal network).

1.3.4 *Rightness.* When requestors initiate a request with a person they do not know, they often justify their legitimacy. This usually takes the form of naming a reference or stating one's position in the organization as in Example 56.

(56) Mike: I was given your name by Sid Taylor at Bermuda. Sid says you are a VM expert and would know with whom we should be discussing this.

When I sent out E-mail asking people to participate in my questionnaire on E-mail and E-message facilities, I established the rightness claim by prefacing the request as in Example 57.

(57) I am conducting an analysis of people's use of computer mail and messages within IBM for my doctoral dissertation at Stanford University. I am under contract to IBM and report to Jim Jordan at the Los Angeles Scientific Center.

### 1.4 *Multiple validity claims*

Justification can be used to establish more than one validity claim as in Example 58. Mary establishes both the sincerity claim ("I know you're not going to believe this") and the truth claim ("I need more disk space").

(58) Mary: I know you're not going to believe this, but I need more disk space!!!

## 1.5 *Justification as pre-sequence*

These examples of pre-establishing the conditions for conversation can be considered a type of pre-sequences (for example, Schegloff 1972). All four conditions can be established, whatever the pre-sequence. If, for example, the pre-invitation "What are you doing over the holidays?" is uttered by someone the addressee does not expect an invitation from, the addressee can question the condition of rightness, by asking "Why? What do you want to know for?" or by interpreting the utterance as a direct speech act and therefore listing all his/her plans for the holidays, and precluding an actual invitation s/he may have been delighted to accept. The invitor, therefore, can pre-establish the condition of rightness, saying "I've been wanting to invite you over, but I've been too busy. What are you doing over the holidays?" The four validity conditions, then, are more general principles than specific pre-sequences such as pre-requests, pre-invitations, etc. As claimed above, they can be invoked by the addressee or pre-established by the addresser at any node in the negotiate action network. Since refusals are dispreferred, not only are pre-requests followed by compliance preferred (as Levinson 1983 claims) but pre-requests that establish the validity conditions if these are in doubt are preferred over those that do not. Such pre-requests may include interactional pessimism (Brown and Levinson 1979) as in Example 58 when Mary established her sincerity.

## 1.6 *The effects of medium*

While this model of workplace requests is not medium specific, certain choices are more typical of one medium than another. Thus, for example, while many initial requests are made through CmC, negotiations of the conditions are often made on the telephone or face-to-face. Similarly, while many CmC requests are justified, they are more likely to be justified in face-to-face or telephone conversations. Often, CmC (especially E-message) is used as a pre-request, the requestor sending an E-message asking "You there?" or "Can I call you?" Several conventions are emerging among this community. To avoid refusals, many interactants use a brief E-message, usually "Hi" or "You there?", whose function is similar to the use of the telephone ring as a summons; it is an efficient check to determine whether the potential requestee is logged on and willing to talk. The conventional responses if the requestee is logged on and willing to talk are "Hi" and "Yes". If the requestee is not logged on, the requestor receives a system message indicating that, and also sometimes where the person can be contacted or when s/he will return. If the requestee is logged on, but does not wish to talk, the response is either an apology or absence of any response, the latter being the more common. Silence in this case means "I cannot talk for now" and is not considered rude.

As with most aspects of language, validity claims provide both a background against which speech acts operate and themselves alter the nature of the interaction. From the above discussion, we can see how validity claims operate actively in negotiating requests in a business environment. They operate within a framework of interpersonal relations and can be drawn on to establish interpersonal relations. Examining these claims allows us to see the two-tier nature of interaction: participants respond to both the implicatures and the illocutionary force of an utterance. Although speech act theory addresses the issue of multiple meanings of an utterance and the cooperative principles on which conversation is based, it does not focus on the sequencing of utterances in an interaction, which is the main focus of conversation analysis. To understand how people in the work environment converse for action, it is not sufficient to understand the felicity conditions of a particular speech act, whether direct or indirect. Nor is it sufficient to examine what can fill sequence slots without understanding the general principles that govern the way such slots are filled. By drawing on both approaches to language use in this analysis, I have shown how requests are made and negotiated in this specific work environment.

Chapter 10 and this chapter show that people make a request implicitly or explicitly and the requestee either complies with the request, refuses the request, promises to do it, or refuses the bid on the grounds that one or more of the validity conditions have not been met. In order to prevent such bid refusals, many interactants choose to pre-establish their validity claims explicitly. This option is chosen if (i) the requestor knows the requestee does not share essential relevant background information, such as that s/he has the authority to ask people to respond to a questionnaire; (ii) if the requestor wants to change an aspect of the situation (especially interpersonal relations) that is currently shared knowledge, such as when a manager deliberately wants to reduce institutional power and establish positive, friendly affect with the requestee; or (iii) if the requestor does not know what background knowledge is shared with the requestee. This latter situation can, however, result in Grice's maxim of quantity being flouted if the requestor assumes the knowledge may not be shared when in fact it is and vice versa. Such justifications occur primarily with interactants who have had little contact or between novices and experts. Typically, novice computer users under specify in a request and experts over specify in their responses to novices.

If the requestor does not pre-establish the claims the requestee can refuse the bid, thereby putting the initial request on hold, and question one or more of the validity claims. This subroutine may be entered many times to reach agreement, impasse or a change in the initial request. A refusal of the bid is not a refusal to comply with the request. When a requestee refuses to comply with the request, s/he is agreeing that the request is comprehensible, true, sincere, and right but either cannot or will not perform it. Once the validity claims have been negotiated to the satisfaction of all interactants, the requestee can respond to the initial request by either complying, refusing to comply or promising to comply. If the interactants cannot reach agreement on the validity claims, the initial request can either be aborted or put on hold for further negotiations by the interactants or by others. Thus, when some of the people I requested to fill out questionnaires questioned my rightness claim, despite my pre-establishing it, the negotiation moved to others, in this case management.

In this model, to capture the dynamic and optional nature of conversations, conversations are represented as sequence slots that can be filled by different speech acts, depending on the context of situation. Thus, conversation for action is described as a transition network, with options at each node expressed as system networks, while the options themselves are described as speech acts.

To demonstrate how this model can be applied to discourse, Chapter 12 takes one lengthy exchange in which Les and a colleague jointly solve a problem and analyzes it in detail.

# Chapter 12

# COLLABORATIVE INFORMATION DEVELOPMENT

One recurring subset of conversation for action within this community is conversations in which the participants say they "solve problems". Research into human problem-solving has been one of the major foci of cognitive science (for example Newell and Simon 1972; Fikes and Nilsson 1971). For researchers in this field, problem-solving is the rational choice made from among possible solutions by comparing the outcomes of each and deciding on the most appropriate. This approach operationalizes problem-solving for the purposes of understanding human thought processes and thereby developing computer models that can "solve problems". Underlying this view are assumptions that humans are representable as information processing systems and that they make rational decisions based on plans developed to reach specific goals. Most of this work, however, has involved individuals in simple, small worlds performing physical actions.

How do interactants solve problems interactively through conversation? Conversation as plan-based behavior (for example Grosz 1977; Hobbs and Evans 1980) has been proposed as a framework for analyzing conversation. This approach suggests developing formalisms for classifying common participant goals; for identifying participant actions; for describing conversational strategies; and for classifying genres. The approach, however, like all the work in cognitive science, adopts a cognitive stance; it interprets the possible mental representations and processes participants in a conversation employ. This approach is in contrast to that taken by ethnomethodologists (for example Sacks, Schegloff and Jefferson 1974) and many anthropologists (for example Irvine 1982), for whom conversation is a social object, and discourse types and rules are culturally defined. Sociolinguists (for example Gumperz 1979), however, often take a middle ground: they refer to participant goals and beliefs as reflected in their language use, but do not ascribe intentionality to these goals or claim their analyses have psychological reality. In this chapter I will continue to adopt this intermediate position, one in which the text is the focal point for analysis.

What are the problems Les is asked to solve? He receives many requests for help, from simple requests for information such as

(59a) MSG FROM JOHN: WHAT DOES ACIS STAND FOR?

with simple informs in response:

(59b) msg john academic information services

to lengthy interchanges taking place over several days and often several modes as Les tries to find a solution, goes back to get more information from the requestor, and works on the problem further until some resolution is agreed upon. In other words, Les solves problems through conversations for action.

Thus, the conversation for action comprises several genres whose structures achieve object transmission, information transmission, direction, and information development. These can be classified as genres according to Ferguson's definition: they are conventionalized units of discourse which differ from each other in form, content and use. Information transmission and information development are preliminaries to action. The initiator does not have the information necessary to act. The action may be the response to a request or may be part of the broader institutional conversation for action in which the initiator is engaged. This chapter focuses on information development but, before moving to a detailed description of this genre, I will briefly explain the form, content and use of the others.

1. *Object transmission.* Les receives many requests for programs he has recently updated such as

(60) I need the DUMP package, for some CMSie things. Please send ASAP. (sent as E-mail)

Or, as in the following example, he receives a request for computer tapes with a program on them. Herb has developed a program which Les needs for Projects SEND and FALCON. Although it is not yet ready for production, has not been fully tested and has bugs, Herb has agreed to send it to Les and let Simon and Don test it and make their own modifications. He has sent the program on tape for security reasons and now wants the tapes back for their own backup at Pippin Lab.

(61) FROM PIPVM(HERB): have you sent the tapes back yet? we need them
FROM PIPVM(HERB): .. desparately
FROM PIPVM(HERB): would you please send them federal express today?

Simon and Don have already copied the program onto disk, so they make their own backup copy on tape and Les sends the originals back to Herb.
2. *Direction*. John asks Les to alter some foils for a presentation Les is to make to the President of the Division (Weis) he and John work for. Terry is the Director of Park Lab.

(62) MSG FROM JOHN: CAN YOU CLEAN UP A COUPLE LINES ON THAT FOIL.??
MSG FROM JOHN: ONLY NEED VERY BRIEF BULLIT[21] ITEMS. WEIS WILL SEE ONLY 10 SECONDS OF IT.
MSG FROM JOHN: OR ANYWAY, THATS WHAT TERRY THINKS.

John then sends the annotated foil file back to Les. Les edits the foil file and sends it back to John, who responds:

(63) MSG FROM JOHN: THANKS . . THAT SHOULD DO THE TRICK!

3. *Information transmission*. Sometimes the request coming to (or sent by) Les is for information. This can be a simple request and inform such as in Example 13 earlier (reproduced here in part).

(64) msg elmvm ted i can't find the pid maclibs on the cms/sp3 source disks
msg elmvm ted in building A . . . everything else appears to be there
FROM ELMVM(TED): . . . they're on cmssp 3 290 (pid) disk

Sometimes, the inform is a complex explanation as when Mary asks Peter for information:

(65a) Date: 22 April 1985, 11:32:59 PST
From: Mary Wallace Tie-line 999-9999 MARY at PARKVM
To: PETER at MSNVM
Subject: file too big to edit
My latest Dump file on my A disk is evidently too big to edit. I get error msg that says that.
When you have time, can you send mail to tell me what to do.
Thanks.

She receives the following E-mail from Peter:

(65b) Date: 22 April 1985, 12:05:44 PST
From: P.J.Monroe 9-999-9999 PETER at MSNVM
To: MARY at PARKVM
Subj: Editing Large Files
You need more virtual storage. You can find out what it is by doing:
CP Q V STOR

> You can then try defining a large storage size by doing:
> CP DEF STOR 2M
> (for example 2M if your current store is 1M = 1024K).
> If that takes (you get bounced into CP), you have to IPL CMS again.
> If that does not work, contact Don or Simon and have them increase your virtual memory in the directory.

This inform uses multiple threads of discourse and conditional statements, indicating alternative solutions to the problem (as identified by Black et al. 1983).

As identified in Chapter 10, inform can take the form (or include) traditional genres such as narrative, descriptor, or exposition. In a discussion I had with a colleague about the use and nature of fora, he recounted the following. "In this forum, we were having quite a heated discussion about line length of data in files going across the network ... people had made various comments about what was wrong and what was right and what caused the length to be as it is ... suddenly, Les Stretton appended the forum (he had not participated up to this time) ... he's like the grandfather of VM and he told us the whole history of the network and how, historically, the line length is what it is today ... it had nothing to do with all the reasons we had been proposing ... but, as Les told us, it was established that way in the past because of various hardware and software constraints ... but they no longer exist ... but that's why it's the way it is." This colleague then showed me the forum and I read Les's contribution. It was a narrative, with events arranged in a temporal and causal sequence to form a story line with a complication, resolution and evaluation as identified by researchers in narrative structure (for example, Rumelhart 1975; van Dijk 1977; de Beaugrande 1984).

On other occasions, the inform is a description of a piece of equipment or an account of how a program or a machine works.

4. *Collaborative information development*. Often the problem requires collaboration before a resolution is reached. As noted earlier in Chapter 9, in accounting for the structure of exchanges of information, Berry (1981) has proposed three layers of structure: an interpersonal layer, a textual layer, and an ideational layer. The interpersonal layer involves a primary knower and secondary knower whose contributions to the discourse are ordered, some being obligatory and others being optional. Each contribution has optional realizations. The textual layer accounts for the way turns are taken and the ideational layer accounts for the organization of propositions. In other words, the three layers refer to knower, speaker and information. While this characterization accounts for the genre I have called information transmission, it does not account for the genre collaborative information development. This

genre has an emergent quality as participants change knower roles. The remainder of this chapter explores the way participants collaborate to develop new information, the way knower roles emerge during the course of the conversation, and the way the conversation cycles differently through the network of conversation for action. The following example illustrates this genre. It is a typical example of problem solving in the VM community.

To get their work done, program developers depend on help from colleagues. During the development stage, they rely on exchange of ideas and information; during the ad tech stage (when the program is tested internally), they rely on data center managers to agree to test the program and then on the system programmers to report bugs and even write their own fixes; once the program is a company product, they rely on both customers and internal users to report bugs and again, often provide their own fixes.[22] Although a team is ultimately responsible for the quality and support of a product, the nature of the product is the result of a long period of cross-fertilization from a variety of sources. The following example fits into this typical pattern. Les has developed code which is at the ad tech stage and he is expecting and receiving input from colleagues in various locations. Like most such conversations, it takes place within a setting of commitment to achieving a reliable and functionally useful product.

This example is a lengthy exchange between Les (L) and Herb (H) using E-messages. For convenience of reading, I have omitted the system command and node and have identified each E-message with the name of the sender: Herb's E-messages are in mixed case, the default at Pippin Lab. The discussion concerns the code for project ROBIN and involves four separate parts of the code: DMSERD, ACM, ACF, and FOR. Prior to the discussion of the problem reported here, Les and Herb had exchanged E-mail and sent each other files.

> 1/10/85: Herb tells Les he has found a bug in the ROBIN program. Later the same day, he tells Les of another bug and sends him a fix that he has made to the code which solves the problem. Still later the same day, he sends Les another piece of E-mail to say he has written a fix for the first problem, which he also sends to Les.
> 1/11/85: Herb sends Les another piece of E-mail describing another bug and a fix he's written. He sends the fix to Les.

Les applies these three fixes to his source code and sends the new version to several colleagues. On February 4th, Herb tells Les they are still having problems and the following conversation takes place.

```
(66a) H1:   We are having trubble (now that I applied your fixes)
      H2:   .. with RECFM V files that are appended to. CMS dies
      H3:   .. trying to read them
      H4:   Example case is trying to append to a mail log ..
```

H5: The writes appear to work (no error codes returned)
H6: .. but an attempt to read them sends CMS to the CPU
H7: .. in the sky...

Herb received no response to these E-messages because Les was involved in a lengthy exchange of E-messages with Simon. He therefore sent the following E-message.

(66b) H8: Pls acknowledge msgs...

Les continues his conversation with Simon (21 E-messages) before replying to Herb:

(66c) L1: ... hopefully my changes correspond to the ones you listed in prior message to me
L2: except for dmserd robin2 which should catch a 'failure' case
L3: ... i.e. it is possible that dmserd robin2 doesn't completely solve the problem
L4: but for the case that the update traps for ... there should be a failure in any case
L5: for the other updates, it may be possible that i didn't correctly translate
L6: your english discription of the fixes .... but i haven't had any failures in the tests i've run
L7: ... sorry i didn't reply sooner, but was in the middle of doing something else.
H9: no problem. Anyway, I hadn't had any failures with my
H10: .. fixes either until I put your new DMSERD ROBIN1
H11: ... and ROBIN2
H12: fixes on ..
H13: The DMSERD ROBIN1 update was smaller than the one
H14: .. it replaced. I don't have the old one anymore so I
H15: .. can't backtrack...
L8: the new robin1 is suppose to be functionally equivalent to what your prior memo described
L9: ... i.e. changes only for those things you described
H16: What memo ?? I didn't send any fixes for DMSERD...
H17: .. Only for ACM, ACF and FOR...
L10: oops sorry, let me double check
H18: Hmm, the DMSERD you just sent is different from the
H19: .. one you sent the other day...
L11: it is the old one, doing diff of the two right now

Les then uses a program to compare the two files and finds that the two files are different. Several minutes pass because while Les is doing this, he receives more E-messages from Simon, continuing their conversation (for 76 E-messages). Finally, Herb asks

(66d) H20: Find out anything interesting ??

and Les responds

(66e) L12: dmserd gull1 that i sent last week was missing two fixes
L13: i'm not sure how the mix-up occured, but the 'old' version should be correct
H21: GULL1 or ROBIN1 ??
L14: dmserd robin1 was missing two fixes
H22: Ok, thanks. I'll put the old one back and see what
H23: .. happens . . .
L15: the 218 record robin1 was correct, don't know how 211 version had later date
L16: the oct, 84, 218 record version had two fixes w/o sid numbers
L17: while the majority of the records in the file had robin1 sid
L18: the file sent last week with 211 records had a later date was missing the 'fixed' lines
L19: i don't know how mixup occured yet . . . other than i have source located at 3 different locations
L20: but that doesn't account for date being later
H24: Blame it on little magical gremelins. . .

Les then sends E-mail to Herb and several other colleagues to whom he had sent the incorrect file, telling them the most recent file did not have essential fixes:

(66f) re: dmserd robin1; the "new" dmserd robin1 sent out last week was in error. It had a later date but 7 fewer records (211 verses 218) than a "fixed" version. The seven records represented two "fixes" that were done last Oct. . . . the "newer" version was dated in Dec. but was missing the fixes. Fortunately, the "bad, new" version only resided at one of the three local nodes that have the source (out of synch data base may have caused the problem).

The problem arises because Les accidentally applies the three fixes from Herb to an old version of the program, which had a bug in it. When Herb tries to run it, he comes across this bug and tells Les (H1–H7). Les assumes there is some problem with the three new fixes and replies accordingly (L1–L7). Herb then tells him that his own three fixes on the old version worked fine and the problem only arose with the new file Les sent (H9–12). H13–15 in fact provide what turns out to be vital information, but Les continues with his explanation of what he had done in response to Herb's previous E-mail (memo) in L8–9. "Memo" provides the clue for Herb, who says (H6–7) the fixes he sent were for three other sections of the code, not the one he is now having trouble with (DMSERD). Les checks through all his files with parts of the program and sends Herb a copy of the old version, because Herb has said he doesn't have the old version that worked (H14–15). Herb repeats (but in different form) what he said in H13, that the two versions are different. Les then runs the comparison program to see what the difference is. When doing this, he discovers that the latest version he has sent out to people is shorter because it does not have two previous fixes. Thus, when Herb tried to run it with his three new fixes, it was the old bug that caused the program to fail. Les then tries to understand how he made this error (L15–20).

## 1. Structure of collaborative information development

### 1.1 *Action structure*

The E-message interaction is an episode, the whole conversation beginning with Les sending out updates of the SEND program (which is an implicit request for people to run the program, find bugs, apply fixes and/or report the bugs to Les). This episode is one of many embedded within the larger framework of institutional conversations for innovation and product development. The larger request for the complete debugging of SEND is not met in this episode, and, by the very nature of computer programming, will never be completely realized. Thus, for practical reasons of analysis, I will examine the episode which begins with an initial request, which is resolved in this episode, while keeping in mind that this is only one of many such recurring episodes which advance the larger institutional conversation.

1. action bid (H1–7)
2. bid refuse (silence)
3. action bid (H8) to meet validity condition of sincerity
4. action (L1–6)
5. action (L7)
6. action accept (H9)
7. action bid (H9–15)
8. action (L8–9)
9. action bid (H16–17)
10. action (L10)
11. action (file sent)
12. action accept (H18)
13. action bid (H18–19)
14. action (L11)

15. action (L11)
16. action bid (H20)
17. action (L12–13)
18. action bid (H21)
19. action (L14)
20. action accept (H22–23)
21. action (L15–20)
22. action accept (H24)

We can see that, to develop information collaboratively, Les and Herb cycle through several action bid/action structures. How is this structure realized through language?

1. Action bid (H1–7) is realized by an implicit request, an assert.
2. Bid refuse is an example of speaker and hearer differently interpreting silence. Herb becomes impatient and so initiates another request, this time an explicit request action bid. Les, however, was busy and used silence as a delaying tactic, not a refusal of the bid.
3. Action bid (H8) is realized by an explicit request, an ask to negotiate the validity condition of sincerity
4. Action (L1–6) is realized by a series of asserts creating an inform. One, "i haven't had any failures in the tests i've run" can also be considered an action bid because Herb responds with a matching assert (H9).
5. Action (L1–7) is realized by an implicit non-speech act (the actual sending of E-messages, followed by an express (L7) with an assert as explanation.
6. Action accept (H9) is realized by a declare in response to Les's express, thus ending the embedded conversation requesting interaction.
7. Action bid (H9–15) is realized by four asserts. The first responds to an implicit action bid by Les (L6), the next two repeat the former action bid (H1–7) and the last is an implicit request for a copy of the old file. We can make this claim because Les responds to it as a request by sending Herb the file.
8. Action (L8–9) is realized by two asserts which repeat the information in the previous action (L1–7) that Herb did not accept.
9. Action bid (H16–17) is realized by an explicit request, the question "What memo??" and an implicit one, the assert of inform. Herb requests clarification because from his point of view, the validity condition of truth has not been met.
10. Action (L10) is realized by an explicit promise, "let me double check", framed in an express.
11. Action is an implicit non-speech act, that is, Les sends Herb a file, in response to his assert that "I don't have the old one anymore so I can't backtrack".

12. Action accept (H18) is realized by an implicit speech act, an assert ("the DMSERD you just sent"). But the same sentence involves another speech act in the predicate.
13. Action bid (H18–19) is realized by implicit speech act, an assert.
14. Action (L11) is realized by an explicit assert of an inform ("it is the old one") in reply to Herb's query of why the two files are different.
15. Action (L11) is realized by an implicit promise, an inform ("doing the diff right now") which implies Les will tell Herb the results of the "diff."
16. Action bid (H20) is realized by an explicit request, a question.
17. Action (L12–13) is realized by three asserts.
18. Action bid (H21) is realized by an explicit request, a question. Herb requests clarification because from his point of view, the validity condition of truth has not been met.
19. Action (L14) is realized by an implicit speech act, an assert in response to action bid in H21.
20. Action accept (H22–23) is realized by close bid with a pre-close (ok), a declare (thanks) and a promise. The promise leaves the conversation open; Herb has accepted the action with a condition.
21. Action (L15–20) is realized by a series of asserts as Les informs Herb of his interpretation of what happened.
22. Action accept (H24) is realized by an amusing declare.

### 1.2 *Participant structure*

Because this episode is collaborative information development, I have adapted Berry's notion of primary and secondary knower to illustrate how these participant roles alternate to produce collaboration and development of information. I will use PK and SK to indicate which interactant fills this role at each speech act in the structure. The participant structure is identified in the summary chart of Conversation for Information Development (Figure 23).

When Herb becomes the primary knower, there is a turn in the conversation. Until then, Les assumed he had the information and the program should work the way he describes it. When Herb becomes primary knower, Les has to re-evaluate his information, adding Herb's new information and trying to become primary knower again. However, Herb is still in the role of primary knower because he knows the two files are different (which he knew before, but which Les did not acknowledge). Again, he takes the role of primary knower by questioning which file Les is referring to (H21). In the final speech act, Herb takes both roles: he accepts Les's role as primary knower in general, but also takes an amusing role of primary knower of the causes of the problem. One of the reasons this problem takes so long to resolve is the initial stance taken by both interactants. Herb takes the role of secondary knower and Les that of primary knower, which matches their interpersonal roles of Les as expert. In fact, Herb had primary knowledge even in his initial request but did not act as primary knower. Even when he is primary knower (H13–14), he never directly confronts Les based on this knowledge. It is only when Les refers to "memo" that Herb asserts his primary knower role and the conversation begins to move towards resolution.

### 1.3 *Conversation for information development*

The chart (Figure 23) summarizes the structure of the conversation in Example 66, indicating the node on the conversation for action network, the surface realization, and the participant structure.

This example illustrates how people work together to create new understanding; how recurring conversations for action provide the vehicle for reaching individual and institutional goals of innovation and product development. It also illustrates how roles held against an institutional background of primary expert and secondary expert can hinder (even if only briefly) the process of solving problems.

The model of conversation for action provides an explanatory tool for analyzing the different genres that recur within this community and the notion of primary and secondary knower provides a tool for examining participant structure to demonstrate how people collaborate to reach mutual resolution through action, against the background of perceived roles.

Figure 23. *Conversation for information development*

| | DIALOGUE | NODE IN TRANSITION NETWORK | REALIZATION | PS |
|---|---|---|---|---|
| H1: | We are having trubble (now that I applied your fixes) | action bid (H1–7) | assert | SK |
| H2: | . . with RECFM V files that are appended to. CMS dies | justification of truthfulness (unmarked) | | |
| H3: | . . trying to read them | | | |
| H4: | Example case is trying to append to a mail log . . | | | |
| H5: | The writes appear to work (no error codes returned) | | | |
| H6: | . . but an attempt to read them sends CMS to the CPU | | | |
| H7: | . . in the sky . . . | | | |
| | | bid refuse | silence | PK |
| H8: | Pls acknowledge msgs . . . | request (H8) explicit | ask | SK |
| | | negotiate validity condition of sincerity | | |
| L1: | . . . hopefully my changes correspond to the ones you listed in prior message to me | action (L1–6)<br>also action response to H8 | assert | PK |
| L2: | except for dmserd robin2 which should catch a 'failure' case | | assert | |
| L3: | . . . i.e. it is possible that dmserd robin2 doesn't completely solve the problem | | assert | |
| L4: | but for the case that the update traps for . . . there should be a failure in any case | | assert | |
| L5: | for the other updates, it may be possible that i didn't correctly translate | | assert | |
| L6: | your english discription of the fixes . . . but i haven't had any failures in the tests i've run | action bid | assert | PK |
| L7: | . . . sorry i didn't reply sooner, | action | express | PK |
| | but was in the middle of doing something else. | justification of bid refuse | | |
| H9: | no problem. | action accept | declare | SK |
| | Anyway, I hadn't had any failures with my | action bid (H9–12) | assert | SK |
| H10: | . . fixes either until I put your new DMSERD ROBIN1 | action bid (repeat) | assert | SK |

*(Figure 23 continued)*

| DIALOGUE | NODE IN TRANSITION NETWORK | REALIZATION | PS |
|---|---|---|---|
| H11: . . . and ROBIN2 | | | |
| H12: fixes on . . | | | |
| H13: The DMSERD ROBIN1 update was smaller than the one | new action bid H13–14 | assert | PK |
| H14: . . it replaced. I don't have the old one anymore so I | new action bid H14–15 | assert | PK |
| H15: . . can't backtrack . . . | | | |
| L8: the new robin1 is suppose to be functionally equivalent to what your prior memo described | action (L8–9) | assert | PK |
| L9: . . . i.e. changes only for those things you described | | assert | PK |
| H16: What memo ?? | action bid (H16–17) | request | PK |
| I didn't send any fixes for DMSERD . . . | justification of truthfulness (unmarked) | inform | |
| H17: . . Only for ACM, ACF and FOR . . . | | | |
| L10: oops sorry, | action (L10) | express | SK |
| let me double check | promise (L10) | assert | SK |
| | action (non-speech act) | file sent | |
| H18: Hmm, the DMSERD you just sent | action accept (H18) | assert | SK |
| is different from the | action bid (H18–19) | assert | PK |
| H19: . . one you sent the other day . . . | | | |
| L11: it is the old one, | action | assert | PK |
| doing diff of the two right now | promise | inform | PK |
| H20: Find out anything interesting ?? | action bid | request | SK |
| L12: dmserd gull1 that i sent last week was missing two fixes | action (L12–13) | assert | PK |

*(Figure 23 continued)*

| DIALOGUE | NODE IN TRANSITION NETWORK | REALIZATION | PS |
|---|---|---|---|
| L13: i'm not sure how the mix-up occured, but the 'old' version | | assert | PK |
| should be correct | | assert | PK |
| H21: GULL1 or ROBIN1 ?? | action bid (H21) | request | PK |
| | | | SK |
| L14: dmserd robin1 was missing two fixes | action (L14) | assert | PK |
| H22: Ok, thanks. | action accept (H22–23) | pre-close | SK |
| | | declare | |
| I'll put the old one back and see what | promise | assert | SK |
| H23: . . happens . . . | | | |
| L15: the 218 record robin1 was correct, don't know how 211 | action (L15–20) | assert | PK |
| version had later date | | assert | PK |
| L16: the oct, 84, 218 record version had two fixes w/o sid numbers | | assert | PK |
| L17: while the majority of the records in the file had robin1 | | assert | PK |
| | bid | | |
| L18: the file sent last week with 211 records had a later date | | assert | PK |
| was missing the 'fixed' lines | | | |
| L19: i don't know how mixup occured yet . . . other than i have | | assert | PK |
| source located at 3 different locations | | assert | PK |
| L20: but that doesn't account for date being later | | assert | PK |
| H24: Blame it on little magical gremelins . . . | action accept (H24) | declare | SK |
| | | | PK |

# PART IV:
# CONCLUSIONS

This study began by questioning the ways in which new technology, in particular the computer as medium of communication, has affected language and its use and how an understanding of this new medium informs our understanding of language use in general. By identifying "who speaks what language to whom and when?", I demonstrated how Les and his colleagues make use of all the language resources available to them to accommodate communication within their working environment and how they switch modes to adapt to the contexts in which they communicate.

## 1. Literacy

This view of mode as choice suggests new ways of approaching literacy and orality: both in research and in the implementation of literacy programs. Modes of communication are hybrids of literacy and orality and as each bundles literacy practices differently, we need to accept and account for different literacies (as Heath has done, 1983) as they are practiced within a community. The modes that literacy takes are dependent on the context of situation within a given community at a given time. Not only has this new technology broadened the range of communication modes for this community, but also the users have developed strategies for using the technology. They have developed a new literacy practice with its own surface manifestations such as the abbreviations and conventions discussed in Chapter 3. They have learned to interpret silence, how to anticipate their audience, how to take turns and to make communication rather than accuracy of production their prime goal.

Within this study, is a brief exploration of the acquisition of "terminal literacy". Mary learned the conventions of computer communication through both successful and unsuccessful conversations, in particular, the problem of judging the knowledge shared with the audience. Both Mary and her interactants misjudged their knowledge of each other, Mary often assuming they were less tolerant of novices than they actually were and the interactants assuming she knew less or more technically than she did. These data suggest that novice users over-compensate for their lack of skill while experts assume the worst case to avoid constant cycling through the action bid/action network for clarification. A detailed longitudinal study of several novice computer communicators would provide data for developing training software and training courses.

### 1.1 *Literacy and education*

If language use is a web of communication, then literacy programs need to provide a variety of contexts of situation that allow learners to explore multiple paths through this web. This is counter to the theoretical approach that views language events as falling along a continuum, at one end of which is casual conversation and at the other end of which is academic writing. The data from this study suggest that we need to determine the contexts in which learners communicate, simulate such situations (or provide real situations), and provide learners with language experience appropriate to the contexts.

The computer as word-processor is now widely used in composition instruction (see Wresch 1984). The goal in adopting this technology is to improve the writing process and, in particular, revision. However, the computer as medium of communication has not been utilized in composition instruction. The research reported here suggests that providing learners with another mode of communication (in particular, a mode which is a different path through the web of communication than either face-to-face or pen-and-ink) will broaden their range of modes. CmC provides interactivity, but is written. It is relatively unplanned and thus users are freed from over-concentration on error. At the same time, users need to be more explicit than in face-to-face conversation because there are no paralinguistic and non-linguistic cues and there is insufficient time to ask for clarification. In addition, teachers and the media have recognized learners' interest in using this mode of communication. Similarly, CmC provides a truly communicative approach to language learning, very different from the computer-as-drill-master approach in most current software (see Underwood 1984).

Not only does the technology affect language and its use, but also the technology itself is affected. The technology is constantly being updated as a result of improvements in software and hardware and human factors considerations. During this study, I saw the introduction and wide use of mixed-case programs for E-messages, a program for capturing and storing incoming E-messages, and a program for separating incoming E-mail files and storing them separately from other files. The questionnaire and its results provide recommendations for new software in order to adapt the technology to how the community wants to make use of these modes of communication.

## 2. Conversation for action

The model for a conversation for action is based on a broad notion of conversation, developed because conversation is not medium dependent. E-messages are similar to face-to-face conversations. However, conversation cannot be applied only to this mode because many conversations move from E-messages to E-mail to face-to-face to telephone. They may even include pre-set segments such as GONE messages. If episodes written at a computer terminal are part of conversations, then so too are episodes written with traditional pen-and-ink or print. Letters, notes and documents can also be episodes in a conversation. This then raises the question of the status of modes such as lectures, journal articles, newspaper reports, and so on. Although the amount of interactivity varies across these modes, they are part of ongoing human communication through language; they are requests for action or asserts through informs, expressives etc.

These data, then, move us away from folk notions of conversation and also away from ethnomethodological ones with openings, closings and turn-taking. Speech act theory, with its view of language as action, provided a useful basis for examining these data. Speech act theory itself, however, is concerned with individual utterances and their effect, not with an overall pattern for conversation. Winograd and Flores provided this more global view by considering conversation for action; by identifying the overall goal of conversations in the business community. However, when we seek to identify other possible conversations, we find only one other genre is possible, chat. Chat differs from conversation for action because it does not change the current state of affairs. Although language use can be broadly divided into these two categories, I also identified another category, unfocused (see Chapter 5). From the point of view of the sender, the episode may be the initiation of either conversation for action or conversation for social maintenance. However, the receivers may respond with "what am I supposed to do with this?", that is, ask to renegotiate the validity condition of sincerity. The way the sender responds to their request will then determine whether the episode initiates conversation for action or conversation for social maintenance. On the other hand, in contexts of situation with little opportunity for interactivity, such renegotiation may be a-typical and the episode's status therefore may remain unfocused.

This model is a first step in understanding both the way interactants negotiate the conditions of conversation in a business environment and how CmC has become incorporated as an additional medium of communication. Several issues need further exploration in order to verify and expand this model. In particular, future studies need to determine who uses justification to whom and when, and who questions the validity conditions of a request by whom and when. To do this, such studies must test the model against data from other work environments, both with and without CmC, and examine the effects of medium, situation, and interpersonal relations in more detail. Such an expanded model would then serve as a valuable theoretical foundation for the practice of personal interactions in the work environment.

By examining the recurring conversations for action and, in particular, collaborative information development, I showed how the community uses language to reach individual and institutional goals of innovation and product development. Further, the models of conversation developed here provide a starting point for analyzing data in other communities, with or without computer-mediated communication, when the particulars of "who speaks what language to whom, and when?" are different.

## 2.2 *Other contexts*

Applied to a more formal setting, in which the interactants' roles were institutionalized hierarchically, we might find different patterns and paths through the networks. In classroom settings, for example, we could see how (and if) knowledge is developed through collaborative strategies; do classrooms provide settings in which students can be primary knowers or in which cycles of action bid/action discourses provide the vehicle for opening up new possibilities of interaction and information? In settings in which roles are even less defined than in the data presented here, in which knowers and expertise are the same, what differences would we find? In family settings, what form do conversations for action take? Which genres are the most common? We could ask similar questions for different cultures. What paths through the networks are preferred in different cultures? Are requests primarily realized as implicit speech acts in some cultures? By comparing and contrasting prototypical conversations for action for different contexts of situation, we can explain misunderstandings. In these data the prototypical request is a question with no modality (e.g. "What does ACIS stand for?"). In a context of situation in which the prototypical request is an implicit expressive framed in an inform, we would expect the direct question to be misunderstood, at least at the interpersonal level. Similarly, the absence or presence of an assert or a declare will vary across different contexts. So, too, will the number of cycles through the network to achieve object transmission and the other genres.

This model also provides a useful focus for examining language use at the broadest interpretation of conversation, that is, academic knowledge work. Is the publication of an article in a journal a request opening a new conversation or is it a request seeking to renegotiate validity conditions of truth or comprehensibility or is it an assert realized as an inform? If we traced the path of an argument or topic through journals in this manner, we would have a clear view of how information develops collaboratively, of how primary and secondary knowers change over time, and of the prototypical path through the network. As I suggested earlier, the condition of sincerity is probably assumed and therefore seldom renegotiated. This framework, then, provides a model for exploring language use in any community.

### 2.3 *Computer tools*

This framework also provides a model for building computer tools to handle E-mail and E-message interactions as episodes or conversations. Such tools could help users organize their communications so they know what conversations are unfinished and what still needs to be done to complete them (e.g. Flores' PC-based tool which coaches the user to assign his/her communications explicitly). However, any such coordinator needs to address the issues developing from the data reported here. The surface form of a request, promise, etc. depends on the context of situation. Many users do not want to make their requests sound like commands. Accidental encounters and incidental information can be stepping stones to collaborative information development. Conversations take place across modes. Therefore, any tools designed to manage human communication must be sufficiently flexible to allow individual conversational styles, and to address the web of communication.

Such a tool would need to provide jotting space where users can input requests, etc. via other modes. It would also have periodic reminders built into it so that the user is informed (daily, weekly or whatever choice the individual makes) of outstanding requests and promises. These tools could also track conversations by person, topic and location. In this way, the user could be reminded to visit X's office when he's in building 00 to discuss outstanding topic Y. Or when the user begins to write E-mail or an E-message to A, s/he could be reminded that A has promised to find a document but so far it has not arrived. The user then has the choice of asking A if s/he has found the document. The user may choose not to do this because it is too soon after the initial request or s/he knows A is more likely to respond if reminded in a face-to-face conversation. The concept behind such tools is that the computer is an aide memoire, not that it will simulate human interaction.

By examining language use with new technology, I have been able to identify new ways of viewing literacy and a model for conversations in this particular environment. As just indicated, the model needs expansion, in particular a more explicit means for relating other aspects of the context (in addition to power) with the basic transition network. Such expansion will depend on studies conducted in a variety of different contexts so that networks for other salient context features can be developed. Meanwhile, this model does provide discourse analysts with a model that has the features essential to any model that hopes to identify discourse as it is actually used, including

1. the dynamic way conversations develop;
2. incorporating both immediate context and larger context (including institutional and local), attempting to show how features of the context influence each other during conversation;
3. treating the discourse as prime focus, rather than speaker intentions and
4. identifying paradigmatic choices available to participants.

# Appendix A DATA COLLECTION

It began one cold night in October 1983. My husband (Bill) was working at his home terminal after the system had crashed twice and he and his system programmer had just brought it back up. I went into the den to give Bill a cup of coffee when suddenly an E-message flashed across the screen. It was from a friend and colleague who'd noticed the crashes and was offering his help. Bill's fingers flew across the keyboard and off went an E-message. E-messages raced back and forth. As I left the room, an idea began to germinate. Over the next several weeks I talked often with Bill about his perceptions of the use of the computer as a tool for communication. I found that the few moments I had accidentally witnessed were typical of much of his communication. Questions arose in my mind: How were people adapting to this new form of communication? What sort of language did they use? How did they choose among the telephone, face-to-face and computers as their means of communication? How did this affect their language use? I was then in a doctoral program at Stanford University and had a topic for my dissertation already mapped out. However, I was fascinated by this discovery. My advisor, Shirley Heath, was enthusiastic about my studying CmC for my dissertation.

It was clear that an ethnographic study was best suited to answering the questions above. The person to be studied had to meet certain requirements. I needed someone who was facile in using the range of computer communicating facilities, for whom communication was a large part of his/her work and who was willing to participate in the study. The first two criteria were essential. Because this is a first exploration into the language of CmC, it was essential to limit the number of variables by examining the proficient use of CmC. If the subject had been unfamiliar with CmC, the study would have had to include the acquisition of this form of communication. We can only study the acquisition of any language use when we know the target form. Nevertheless, the study of the acquisition of computer-mediated communication is also needed. Therefore, I also tracked my own acquisition of CmC. This acquisition is not the focus of the current research, but it gave me another perspective on language use. Further, because the study reported here focuses on only one person, I wanted both a large quantity of communication and a wide variety of communicators to be able to determine patterns of language use. Thus, although the way people communicate with the subject will be partly dependent on the subject and they may use different language when communicating with other people, I would still be able to get the range of the subject's language use.

I then undertook the task of finding a subject willing to be shadowed for eight months. An IBM manager, Jim Jordan, offered to support the project if I could find a suitable subject. Six months later, after many attempts to find a willing subject, Les Stretton agreed to participate. He, like those who had declined, was concerned that my presence would interfere with his work and affect his relationship with other people. However, he was willing to give it a try. After the first two weeks of constant observation, I asked him if my presence was a problem. The only problem he reported was that he sometimes felt he was neglecting me because he never spoke to me. All was well. After this initial observation period, I made random visits to Les's office to identify any changes from the patterns I had initially recorded. I was given my own office on the same corridor as Les's. I was quickly accepted by Les's colleagues at Park Lab not only as his shadow, but also in my own right because I was often there when Les was at another Lab or on a business trip elsewhere in the country. My role as shadow became eclipsed by my role as computer communications researcher. This role was more firmly established with the distribution of a questionnaire to all of Les's interactants. Les's identity was kept anonymous and only those who work most closely with him either at Park Lab or on one of his projects are aware of my other identity.

The over-arching framework for data collection was ethnographic with the researcher as participant observer. The data set consists of five different types of data: field notes from observations, taped interviews, console logs of all terminal activity, E-mail files, hardcopy artifacts, and questionnaire responses. Initially, observation was for two full working weeks during which period I was able to orient myself to Les's office work patterns. Over the next eight months, observations were carried out randomly. During observation periods, I shared an office with the subject and accompanied him to meetings. I did not interrupt or intrude during interactions. I made notes of questions and necessary elaborations I would ask later at interviews. The subject travels frequently to other IBM locations. I accompanied him on one such trip to compare and contrast his language use in the two different environments.

I kept a journal of observations of all communicative events. (A communicative event is defined here as an interaction between the subject and any incoming language data.) This data originated from different media: the computer terminal, telephone, print, writing, and speech. It included systems messages, written memos, and face-to-face conversations. In addition, journal notes were made of activities that occurred before and after the communicative event and that co-occurred with it, for example checking documentation before sending the information via an E-message. Further, notes were made of the context of all communicative events (e.g. whether the subject was in his office, was seated, or whether other people were present).

Les's console logs form one large data set. A special program logged all Les's terminal activity from Sept. 11, 1984 to May 27, 1985 and then forwarded the logs to me. These logs were then edited for all instances of communication using a specially designed program. The edited logs were used to determine the networks of interactants described in Part I. I wrote further programs to edit these logs for the instances of conversational openings and closings which are discussed in Chapter 10.

Les keeps E-mail on one disk to which he gave me access. These files were also edited for specific instances of language use (such as greetings) using a specially designed program. These files were used to determine the networks of interactants described in Part I.

Hard-copy artifacts include written memos, formal documents, overhead transparencies for presentations, and computer manuals. In addition, as colleagues learned of my study, they gave me copies of newspaper/magazine articles which referenced computer-mediated communication. Other colleagues sent me copies of papers they had written and which had some reference to this new medium of communication.

As part of the process of triangulation, I discussed the data I collected with Les. These discussions included three specific interviews, and many conversations, both face-to-face and on-line. I interviewed Les before the study, after the initial two weeks of intensive observation, and then at the end of the study. These interviews were audio-tape recorded and transcribed. The interview questions were designed to elicit three types of information: (i) Les's perspective on his use of and attitudes to CmC, (ii) his interpretation of communicative events observed, and (iii) clarification of terminology or patterns of computer use shown in the console logs or E-mail files. In the initial interview, I concentrated on Les's view of the computer as medium of communication because I wanted to record his perspective before his views had been influenced in anyway by my study. The interview lasted almost one hour (over two days) because, at this stage in the research, I was a naive computer user and so Les enjoyed teaching me. Although I began with a list of potential questions, many questions were generated interactively as I responded to information Les gave me. The questions included the following:

- How long have you been working in computers?
- What do you use them for?
- When did you first start using them to communicate with colleagues?
- What types of communication do you use?
- There seems to be a multiplicity of systems operating. What ones do you personally favor?

- What sort of information do you communicate using the interactive on-line mode?
- If the technology were available to send something more complex and have immediate receipt, would you be likely to use it?
- Do you find that a problem—of trying to track the conversation?
- As you're talking I kept thinking of maybe the reasons why it's (E-messages) more accepted by people on the technical side rather than on the management side?
- Obviously in your work life you still use the telephone and face-to-face interaction and I wondered what makes you choose between them?

In the other two interviews, I concentrated more on asking Les to interpret communicative events I had observed and to clarify terminology and patterns I had noted in observation notes, in the console logs or in the E-mail file. Therefore, these questions included specifics such as:

- I notice you use an exec (personal program) called "ckmsg". What does that actually do?
- How do you distribute your time between the two terminals?
- How do you find talking on the telephone and working at the terminal? I've noticed you do both (at the same time).
- How often do you use IBM internal mail (hard copy)?

As participant in the work environment, I was also able to talk with Les and his colleagues informally over lunch, after meetings, in the corridors and in their offices. I was especially fortunate to become friends with several old hands who were useful sources of information concerning the early days of interactive computing and computer networking. From them I learned of the exponential growth of the network and its institutional setting.

As colleagues became aware of my interest in CmC, they began sending me copies (soft and hard) of any information they thought might be relevant. At least once a week, I would find an unsolicited piece of E-mail or a document or a forum in my reader. Over lunch colleagues would often recount some incident concerning CmC. To maintain the relaxed collegial atmosphere that prevailed at lunch, I did not take notes. When I returned to my office, I would immediately write down what I had just learned.

As part of my report to IBM, a detailed questionnaire on the use of and the attitudes to computer E-mail and E-message facilities was sent to the 246 colleagues with whom Les had interacted between September 1984 and May 1985 (when the questionnaire was sent out). The questionnaire was designed to answer questions about specific features of the various different E-mail and E-message tools used within IBM. These tools include ones available in IBM products as well as programs written locally to facilitate particular local needs. The questionnaire is not reported on in detail here because it primarily concerns the specifics of editing, receiving and sending in the available tools. These details are not the focus of this book; however, part of the questionnaire refers to general questions on the use of CmC. These questions include asking who they communicate with using a particular tool; how many people they communicate with and where those people are located; asking what form of communication people prefer for different activities; how soon they respond to E-mail and messages; how soon they expect a response to their E-mail and E-messages; whether they find E-messages interruptive; and whether they like people forwarding their E-mail. The responses to the questions confirm the interview data and the observation data reported in Part I (in particular, Chapter 5). For example, people use CmC to their superiors, to technical experts, and to their employees. Their interactants may be in an office in the same hallway or may be in another state or country. Some people have definite preferences for the mode of communication. For instance, several respondents stated that they only use computer messaging for "asking or answering simple, quick questions". Most people preferred face-to-face or telephone conversation for "getting to know someone". Respondents confirmed my observation that silence in response to CmC is ambiguous and an immediate response is not expected. Most respondents agreed that E-messages should not interrupt their terminal session. However, they did want to be informed that E-mail or E-messages had arrived. People's responses to the question of forwarding E-mail were divided. The majority, however, accepted that their E-mail was a public document and they wrote it with the knowledge that it might have a wider audience than the person/people to whom they actually sent it. They usually indicate that a particular piece of E-mail should not be forwarded by writing "Personal and Confidential—for your eyes only". A minority felt that E-mail should never be forwarded without the explicit consent of the original writer. Some even wanted to make it technically impossible to forward someone's E-mail. Several technical experts have told me this latter suggestion is technically impossible: no matter what restrictions are placed on sending and receiving, if a person can read the E-mail, s/he can always find a way to copy and re-send it.

Over the course of the eight months' participant observation, I collected and read many fora. As colleagues learned of my study, they forwarded actual fora or references to fora in which they thought I might be interested. These included both theoretical and practical discussions related to CmC.

## Appendix B FLOOR PLAN OF PARK LAB

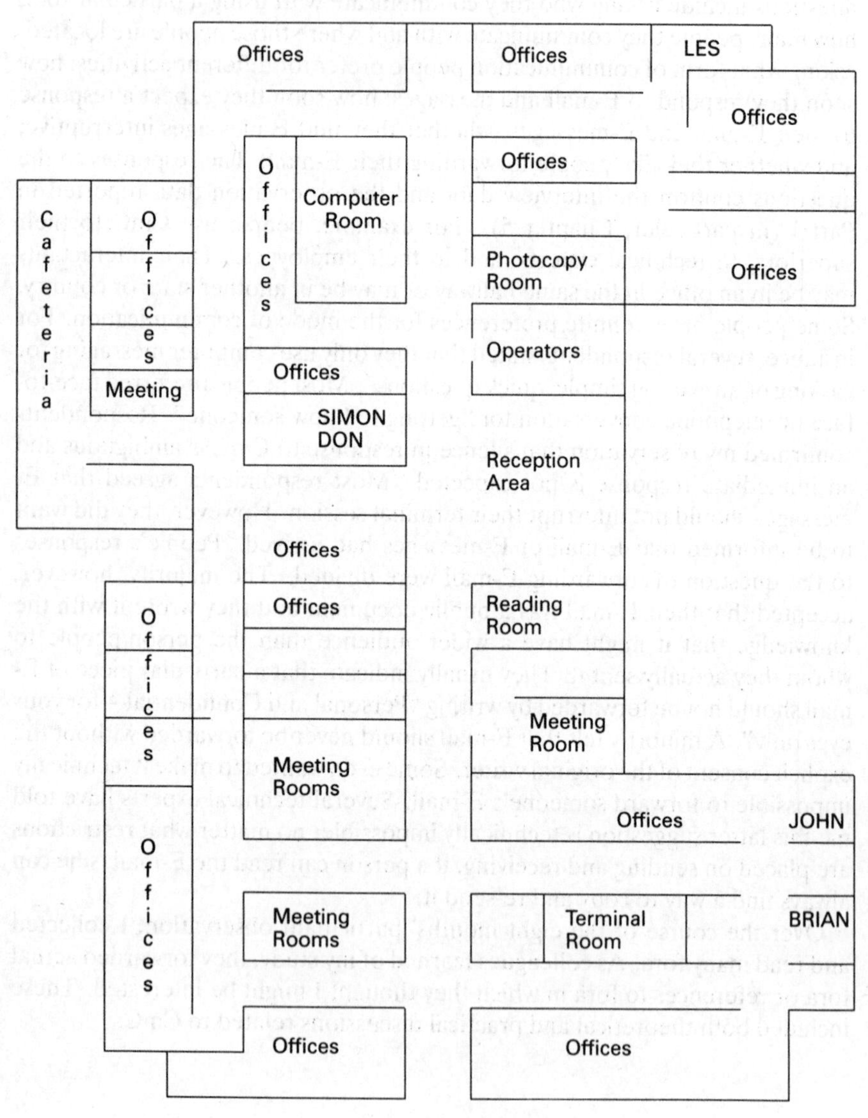

# Appendix C FLOOR PLAN OF LES'S OFFICE

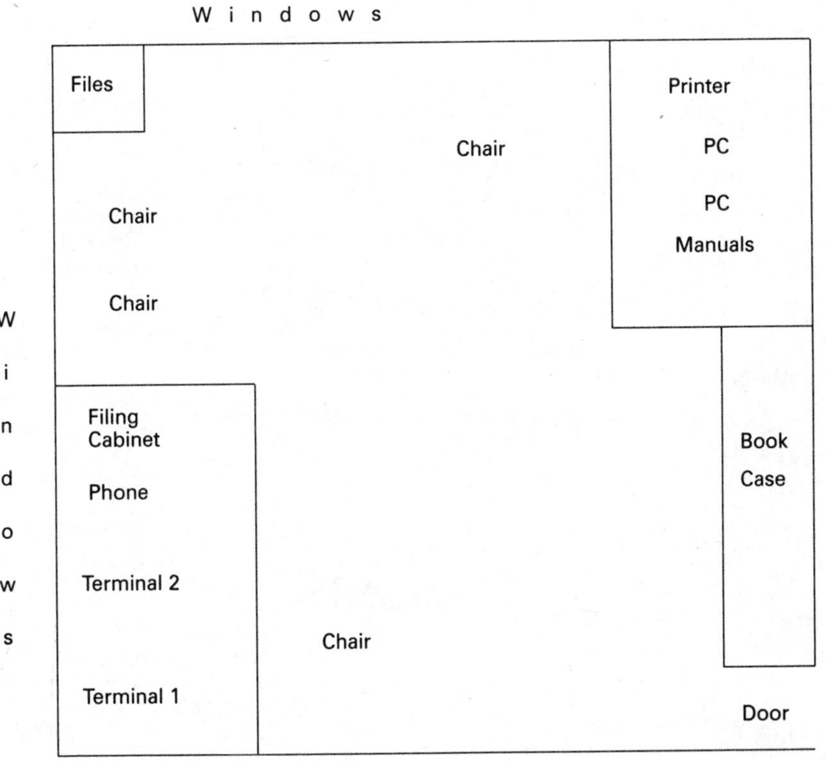

# NOTES

1. Pseudonyms are used to protect the identity of people, IBM locations and projects.
2. Network node is the electronic 'address' of a computer at an IBM location. When there is more than one computer at the same location, each is identified by a number or letter. For example, the two computers at Park are named PARKVM1 and PARKVM2 respectively.
3. Choice will be used interchangeably with use. Neither term implies intentionality or consciousness of choice. Both terms are used here as in systemic linguistics (e.g. Halliday 1973) and by Ervin-Tripp (1972), to emphasize that language use needs to be examined both syntagmatically and paradigmatically.
4. Details of the methodology are in Appendix A.
5. The pseudonyms of participants cited in this study are listed in the Preface.
6. *Code* refers to the contents of a computer program, which is written in a computer language such as Pascal. Programs consist of lines of code. Programs do not always execute precisely as intended because of errors in the code or code that is incompatible with the hardware or other software. Such errors are called *bugs*. If a bug is encountered when a program is running, the program will stop running, and remain in a stalled state, which is referred to as being *hung*.
7. See Appendix B for a floor plan of Park Lab.
8. VM/370/SP is an IBM interactive operating system. VM users/community refers to people who use or write code for the VM system.
9. Fulist refers to a command for calling up a list of all files on the user's disk.
10. PF keys are a set of 12 or 24 keys set for a particular function. By pressing the appropriate key, the user issues a command to the computer. PF keys are assigned to often-used commands to save typing time.
11. Locations mentioned elsewhere in the text are referred to by name. Others are referred to simply by general location. Thus, *East Coast 1* refers to a location on the East Coast of the United States that has not been given a specific pseudonym in the rest of the book. *Other US 1* refers to a location in the United States that is neither on the West Coast nor on the East Coast.
12. Parts of Chapters 5, 6 and 7 first appeared in "The context of oral and written language: A framework for mode and medium switching." *Language in Society*, September 1988.
13. ARPANET is the network system used to connect computer users in the military, in universities, and in colleges.
14. I am here using style as it is used in linguistics, not as used in literary studies.

15. Some scholars working in cognitive science and artifical intelligence do focus on the text and have developed models of discourse processing free of intentionality and with a linguistic focus (e.g. Grosz 1977 and Reichman 1987). However, the main thrust of much work on discourse within the AI paradigm has been towards world knowledge and speaker intentions.
16. I owe John Rickford thanks for suggesting the term "episode" which captures my notions of incomplete, but dynamic parts of conversations better than my former term "fragment".
17. The use of bid follows the notion of language as a game, a metaphor which has been used by several scholars, including Farb 1973, Levin and Moore 1977 and Berry 1981.
18. CMS is an IBM operating system running under VM. Here, Simon uses the suffix "-ie" to mean "like".
19. Parts of this chapter first appeared as "Requests at work: Negotiating the conditions for conversation." *Management Communication Quarterly*, 1987 1:1.58–83.
20. SCRIPT is a program which formats documents. The writer inserts special commands or tags that SCRIPT reads and then applies to the formatted version, for example ".ds" is used to format double spaced.
21. Bullit (sic): the large dot (bullet) preceding items listed on a foil or document, e.g. • project SEND
22. Fix refers to any changes made to a program to remove a bug.

# REFERENCES

Atkinson, J. Maxwell and John Heritage (eds)
1985 *Structure of Social Action: Studies in Conversation Analysis*. Cambridge: Cambridge University Press.

Austin, J. L.
1962 *How to Do Things with Words*. Oxford: Clarendon Press.

Bean, John C.
1983 "Computerized word-processing as an aid to revision". *College Composition and Communication* 34:2.146–8.

Beaugrande, Robert de
1984 *Text Production: Toward a Science of Composition*. Norwood, N. J.: Ablex.

Bell, Allan
1984 "Language style as audience design". *Language in Society* 13.145–204.

Berry, Margaret
1981 "Systemic linguistics and discourse analysis: A multi-layered approach to exchange structure". In Malcolm Coulthard and Martin Montgomery (eds.), *Studies in Discourse Analysis*. London: Routledge and Kegan Paul, 120–45.

Black, Steven D., James E. Levin, Hugh Mehan, and Clark N. Quinn
1983 "Real and non-real time interaction: Unraveling multiple threads of discourse". *Discourse Processes* 6.59–75.

Bridwell, Lillian, Parker Johnson, and Stephen Brehe
1989 "Composing and computers: Case studies of experienced writers". In Ann Matsuhashi (ed.), *Writing in Real Time: Modelling Production Processes*. Norwood, N.J.: Ablex, 81–107.

Bridwell, L., P. R. Nancarrow, and D. Ross
1984 "The writing process and the writing machine: Current research on word processors relevant to the teaching of composition". In R. Beach and L. Bridwell (eds.), *New Directions in Composition Research*. New York: Guildford Press, 381–98.

Bridwell, Lillian, G. Sirc, and Robert Brooke
1985 "Revising and computing: Case studies of student writers". In Sarah Freedman (ed.), *The Acquisition of Written Language: Revision and Response*. Norwood, N.J.: Ablex, 172–94.

Brown, R. and A. Gilman
1960 "The pronouns of power and solidarity". In T. A. Sebeok (ed.), *Style in Language*. Cambridge, Mass.: MIT Press, 253–76.

Brown, R. and S. Levinson.

1979 "Social structure, groups and interaction". In K. Scherer and H. Giles (eds.), *Social Markers in Speech*. Cambridge: Cambridge University Press, 291–347.

Buhler, Karl

1934 *Sprachtheorie*. Jena.

Burton, D.

1980 *Dialogue and Discourse*. London: Routledge and Kegan Paul.

Card, S. K., T. P. Moran, and A. Newell

1983 *The Psychology of Human-Computer Interaction*. Hillsdale, New Jersey: Lawrence Erlbaum Associates.

Carey, John

1980 "Paralanguage in computer mediated communication". *Proceedings of the Association for Computational Linguistics*, 61–3.

Case, Donald Owen

1984 "Personal computers: Their adoption and use in information work by professors". Ph. D. dissertation, Stanford University, California.

Chafe, Wallace L.

1982 "Integration and involvement in speaking, writing, and oral literature". In Deborah Tannen (ed.), *Spoken and Written Language: Exploring Orality and Literacy*. Norwood, N. J.: Ablex, 35–53.

Chomsky, N.

1965 *Aspects of the Theory of Syntax*. Cambridge, Mass.: M.I.T.

Cicourel, Aaron V.

1975 "Discourse and text: Cognitive and linguistic processes in studies of social structure". *Versus* 12.33–84.

Collier, Richard M.

1983 "The word-processor and revision strategies". *College Composition and Communication* 34:2.149–55.

Conklin, Nancy Faires

1984 "Literacy in interaction: The use of electronic message systems". Paper presented at LSA Meeting, Baltimore.

Coulthard, Malcolm

1977 *An Introduction to Discourse Analysis*. London: Longmans.

Daiute, Collette A.

1983 "The computer as stylus and audience". *College Composition and Communication* 34:2.134–45.

van Dijk, T. A.

1977 *Text and Context: Explorations in the Semantics and Pragmatics of Discourse*. London: Longman.

1982 "Episodes as units of discourse analysis". In Deborah Tannen (ed.), *Analyzing Discourse: Text and Talk*. Norwood, N. J.: Ablex, 177–95.

van Dijk, T. A. and W. Kintsch

1983 *Strategies of Discourse Comprehension*. New York: Academic Press.

Dreyfus, Hubert L. and Stuart E. Dreyfus
1986 *Mind over Machine*. New York: The Free Press.
Duranti, Allessandro
1986 "Framing discourse in a new medium: Openings in electronic mail". *Quarterly Newsletter of the Laboratory of Comparative Human Cognition* 8:64–71.
Economou, Dorothy
1985 "Collecting and using authentic conversations in ESL migrant classrooms". Paper presented at A.T.E.S.O.L. 4th Summer School, Sydney, Australia.
Edelsky, Carole
1981 "Who's got the floor?" *Language in Society* 10.383–421.
Edmonson, W.
1981 *Spoken Discourse: A Model for Analysis*. London: Longman.
Eisenstein, Elizabeth
1979 *The Printing Press as an Agent of Change: Communications and Cultural Transformations in Early-modern Europe, V.I.* New York: Cambridge University Press.
Ellis, J. and J. Ure
1969 "Language variety: Register". In A. R. Meetham (ed.), *Encyclopedia of Linguistics, Information, and Control*. London: Pergamon Press, 251–9.
Erickson, Frederick
1982 "Money tree, lasagna bush, salt and pepper: Social construction of topical cohesion in a conversation among Italian-Americans". In Deborah Tannen (ed.), *Analyzing Discourse: Text and Talk*. Washington, D.C.: Georgetown University Press, 43–70.
Erickson, Frederick, and Jeffrey Shultz
1982 *The Counselor as Gatekeeper: Social Interactions in Interviews*. New York: Academic Press.
Ervin-Tripp, Susan
1972 "On sociolinguistic rules: Alternation and co-occurrence". In John J. Gumperz and Dell Hymes (eds.), *Directions in Sociolinguistics*. New York: Holt, Rinehart and Winston, 213–50.
Farb, Peter
1973 *Word Play*. London: Bantam.
Ferguson, C. A.
1977 "Baby talk as a simplified register". In C. E. Snow and C. A. Ferguson (eds.), *Talking to Children*. Cambridge: Cambridge University Press, 209–35.
1983 "Sports announcer talk: Syntactic aspects of register variation". *Language in Society* 12.153–72.
1986 "The study of religious discourse". In D. Tannen and J. E. Alatis (eds.), *Georgetown University Round Table on Languages and Linguistics 1985*. Washington, D.C.: Georgetown University Press, 205–13.
Fikes, R. and N. Nilsson
1971 "STRIPS: A new approach to the application of theorem proving to problem solving". *Artificial Intelligence* 2.189–208.

Fillmore, Charles J.
1982 "Ideal readers and real readers". In Deborah Tannen (ed.), *Analyzing Discourse: Text and Talk*. Norwood, N. J.: Ablex, 248–70.

Firth, J. R.
1957 "Personality and language in society". In J. R. Firth, *Papers in Linguistics 1934–1951*. London: Oxford University Press.

Fishman, Joshua A.
1965 "Who speaks what language to whom and when?" *Linguistique* 2.67–88.

Fowler, Alastair
1982 *Kinds of Literature: An Introduction to the Theory of Genres and Mode*. Cambridge, Mass.: Harvard University Press.

Geertz, Clifford
1973 *The Interpretation of Cultures*. New York: Basic Books.

Gibbon, D.
1981 "Idiomaticity and functional variation: A case study of international amateur radio talk". *Language in Society* 10.21–42.

Giles, H.
1980 "Accommodation theory: Some new directions". *York Papers in Linguistics* 9.105–36.

Goffman, Erving
1974 *Frame Analysis*. New York: Harper and Row.

Goody, Jack
1977 *The Domestication of the Savage Mind*. Cambridge: Cambridge University Press.

Goody, Jack, and Ian Watt
1968 "The consequences of literacy". In Jack Goody (ed.), *Literacy in Traditional Societies*. Cambridge: Cambridge University Press, 53–84.

Gregory, H.
1967 "Aspect of varieties differentiation". *Journal of Linguistics* 3.177–98.

Grice, H. P.
1975 "Logic and conversation". In P. Cole and J. L. Morgan (eds.), *Syntax and Semantics 3: Speech Acts*. New York: Academic Press, 41–58.

Grosz, B.
1977 "The representation and use of focus in dialogue understanding". Stanford Research Institute Technical Note 151, SRI International, Menlo Park, California.

Gumperz, J. J.
1971 "Hindi-Punjabi code-switching in Delhi". In J. J. Gumperz (ed.), *Language in Social Groups*. Stanford: Stanford University Press, 205–19.
1979 "The sociolinguistic basis of speech act theory". In J. Boyd and S. Ferrara (eds.), *Speech Act Ten Years After*. Milan: Versus.
1982 *Discourse Strategies*. Cambridge: Cambridge University Press.

Habermas, Jürgen
1979 *Communication and the Evolution of Society*. Boston: Beacon.

Halliday, M. A. K.
1973 *Explorations in the Functions of Language*. London: Edward Arnold.
1978 *Language as Social Semiotic*. London: Edward Arnold.
1985 *Spoken and Written Language*. Deakin University, Vic.: Deakin University Press.
Halliday, M. A. K., A. McIntosh, and P. Strevens
1964 *The Linguistic Sciences and Language Teaching*. London: Longman.
Halpern, Jeanne W. and Sarah Liggett
1984 *Computers and Composing*. Carbondale, Ill.: Southern Illinois University Press.
Hasan, Ruqaiya
1978 "Text in the systemic-functional model". In Wolfgang U. Dressler (ed.), *Current Trends in Textlinguistics*. Berlin: Walter de Gruyter, 228–46.
Haslett, B. J.
1987 *Communication: Strategic Action in Context*. Hillsdale, N. J.: Lawrence Erlbaum.
Haviland, J. B.
1979 "Guugu Yimidhirr brother-in-law language". *Language in Society* 8.365–93.
Heath, Shirley Brice
1983 *Ways with Words*. Cambridge: Cambridge University Press.
1985 "The cross-cultural study of language acquisition". Paper presented at the Seventeenth Annual Child Language Research Forum, Stanford University, California.
Heath, Shirley Brice, and Charlene Thomas
1984 "The achievement of preschool literacy for mother and child". In Hillel Goelman, Antoinette A. Oberg, and Frank Smith (eds.), *Awakening to Literacy*. Exeter, N. H.: Heinemann Educational Books, 55–73.
Heidegger, Martin
1962 *Being and Time*. New York: Harper and Row.
Henzl, V.
1974 "Linguistic register of foreign language instruction". *Language Learning* 32.207–22.
Hildyard, Angela, and David R. Olson
1978 "Memory and inference in the comprehension of written discourse". *Discourse Processes* 1.91–117.
Hiltz, Starr Roxanne
1984 *Online Communities: A Case Study of the Office of the Future*. Norwood, N. J.: Ablex.
Hiltz, Starr Roxanne and Murray Turoff
1978 *The Network Nation: Human Communication via Computer*. Reading, Mass.: Addison-Wesley.
Hobbs, Jerry R. and David Andreoff Evans
1980 "Conversation as planned behavior". *Cognitive Science* 4.349–77.

Hymes, Dell
1972 "The scope of sociolinguistics". In Roger W. Shuy (ed.), *Sociolinguistics: Current Trends and Prospects*. Washington, D.C.: Georgetown University Press, 313–33.

Irvine, Judith T.
1982 "Wolof speech styles and social status". In Richard Bauman and Joel Sherzer (eds.), *Case Studies in the Ethnography of Speaking*. Austin: Southwest Educational Development Laboratory, 2–13.

Jakobson, R.
1960 "Closing statements: Linguistics and poetics". In T. A. Sebeok (ed.), *Style in Language*. Cambridge, Mass.: MIT Press, 350–73.

Jefferson, G.
1974 "Error-correction as an interactional resource". *Language in Society* 3.181–200.

Kiefer, K. E. and C. R. Smith
1983 "Textual analysis with computers: Tests of Bell Laboratories computer software". *Research in the Teaching of English* 17.201–14.

Kiesler, Sara, Jane Seigel, and Timothy W. McGuire
1984 "Social psychological aspects of computer-mediated communication". *American Psychologist* 39:10.1123–34.

Kling, R. and Walt Scacchi
1982 "The web of computing". In Marshall Yovits (ed.), *Advances in Computers*, Volume 21. New York: Academic Press, 1–90.

Labov, W.
1966 *The Social Stratification of English in New York City*. Washington, D.C.: Center for Applied Linguistics.

Labov, William, and David Fanshel
1977 *Therapeutic Discourse*. New York: Academic Press.

Lakoff, Robin Tolmach
1982 "Some of my favorite writers are literate: The mingling of oral and literate strategies in written communication". In Deborah Tannen (ed.), *Spoken and Written Language: Exploring Orality and Literacy*. New Jersey: Ablex, 239–60.

Levin, J. A. and J. A. Moore
1977 "Dialogue-games: Metacommunication structures for natural language interaction". *Cognitive Science* 1.395–420.

Levinson, Stephen C.
1983 *Pragmatics*. Cambridge: Cambridge University Press.

Levodow, Nancy
1980 "Computer conversations: A hybrid of spoken and written English". Paper presented at the Berkeley Sociolinguistic Meeting, Berkeley, California.

Maclay, H. and C. E. Osgood
1959 "Hesitation phenomena in spontaneous English speech". *Word* 15.19–44.

McLuhan, Marshall
1962 *The Gutenberg Galaxy: The Making of Typographic Man*. Toronto: University of Toronto Press.

McTear, M.
1987 *The Articulate Computer*. Oxford: Basil Blackwell.

Malinowski, Bronislaw
1923 "The problem of meaning in primitive languages". In C. K. Ogden and I. A. Richards (eds.), *The Meaning of Meaning*. London: Kegan Paul, 296–336.

Mandelbaum, David G.
1949 *Selected Writings of Edward Sapir in Language, Culture, and Personality*. Berkeley: University of California Press.

Martin, J. R.
1984 "Language, register and genre". In F. Christie (ed.), *Children Writing: Reader*. Geelong: Deaking University Press, 21–30.
1985 "Process and Text: Two aspects of human semiosis". In James D. Benson and William S. Greaves (eds.), *Systemic Prespectives on Discourse*, Volume 1. Norwood, N. J.: Ablex.

Matsuhashi, Ann
1979 "Producing written discourse: A theory-based description of the temporal characteristics of three discourse types from four competent grade 12 writers". Ann Arbor, Mich.: University Microfilms International.

Murray, Denise E.
1985 "Composition as conversation: The computer terminal as medium of communication". In Lee Odell and Dixie Goswami (eds.), *Writing in Nonacademic Settings*. New York: Guilford Press, 205–29.
1986 "Computer-mediated Communication as an Instructional Tool". In *Tenth Western Educational Computing Conference*, CECC.
1987 "Requests at work". *Management Communication Quarterly* 1.58–83.
1988 "The context of oral and written language". *Language in Society* 17.351–73.
1989 "When the medium determines turns: turn-taking in computer conversation". In Hywell Coleman (ed.), *Working with Language*. The Hague: Mouton, 213–23.

Murray, K. M.
1979 *Caught in the Web of Words: James A. H. Murray and the "Oxford English Dictionary"*. Oxford: Oxford University Press.

Newell, Allen, and Herbert A. Simon
1972 *Human Problem Solving*. Englewood Cliffs, N. J.: Prentice-Hall.

Norman, D. and D. Rumelhart
1975 *Explorations in Cognition*. San Francisco: Freeman.

Nystrand, Martin
1982 "Rhetoric's 'audience' and linguistics' 'speech community': Implications for understanding writing, reading, and text". In Martin Nystrand (ed.), *What Writers Know: The Language, Process, and Structure of Written Discourse*. New York: Academic Press, 1–28.

Olson, David R.

1977 "From utterance to text: The bias of language in speech and writing". *Harvard Educational Review* 47.257–81.

1981 "Writing: The divorce of the author from the text". In Barry M. Kroll and Roberta J. Vann (eds.), *Exploring Speaking-Writing Relationships: Connections and Contrasts*. Urbana, Ill: National Council of Teachers of English, 99–110.

Ong, Walter J.

1977 *Interfaces of the Word: Studies in the Evolution of Consciousness and Culture*. Ithaca: Cornell University Press.

1982 *Orality and Literacy: The Technologizing of the Word*. London: Methuen.

Pattison, Robert

1982 *On Literacy*. Oxford: Oxford University Press.

Peyton, Joy Kreeft, and Trent Batson

1986 "Computer networking: Making connections between speech and writing". *ERIC/CLL News Bulletin* 10:1.1–6.

Pratt, Mary Louise

1981 "The short story: The long and short of it". *Poetics* 10.175–194.

Quinn, Clark N., Hugh Mehan, James A. Levin, and Steven D. Black

1983 "Real education in non-real time: The use of electronic message systems for instruction." *Instructional Science* 11.313–27.

Reichman, Rachel

1987 *Getting Computers to Talk Like You and Me*. Cambridge, Mass.: MIT Press.

Rumelhart, D. E.

1975 "Notes on a schema for stories". In D. G. Bobrow and A. Collins (eds.), *Representation and Understanding: Studies in Cognitive Science*. New York: Academic Press, 211–36.

Sacks, H., E. A. Schegloff, and G. Jefferson

1974 "A simplest systematics for the organization of turn-taking for conversation". *Language* 50:4.696–735.

Sankoff, G.

1980 "Language use in multilingual societies: Some alternate approaches". In G. Sankoff, *The Social Life of Language*. Philadelphia: University of Pennsylvania Press, 29–46.

Schank, R. C. and R. Abelson

1977 *Scripts, Plans, Goals and Understanding*. Hillsdale, N.J.: Erlbaum.

Schegloff, E. A.

1972 "Note on conversational practice: Formulating place". In Pier Paolo Giglioli (ed.), *Language and Social Context*. Harmondsworth: Penguin, 95–135.

1976 "Identification and recognition in telephone conversation openings". In G. Psathas (ed.), *Everyday Language: Studies in Ethnomethodology*. New York: Irvington, 23–78.

Schegloff, E. A. and H. Sacks

1973 "Opening up closings". *Semiotica* 7:4.289–327.

Schegloff, E. A., Gail Jefferson, and H. Sacks
1977 "The preference for self-correction in the organization of repair in conversation". *Language* 53.361–82.
Schiffrin, Deborah
1985 "An empirical base for discourse pragmatics". Paper presented at the Stanford Greenberg/Ferguson Lecture Series, Stanford, California.
Schneiderman, B.
1980 *Software Psychology: Human Factors in Computer and Information Systems.* Cambridge, Mass.: Winthrop.
Scollon, Ron, and Suzanne B. K. Scollon
1981 *Narrative, Literacy and Face in Interethnic Communication.* Norwood, N. J.: Ablex.
Scribner, Sylvia, and Michael Cole
1981 *The Psychology of Literacy.* Cambridge, Mass.: Harvard University Press.
Searle, J. R.
1969 *Speech Acts.* Cambridge: Cambridge University Press.
1975 "Indirect speech acts". In P. Cole and J. L. Morgan (eds.), *Syntax and Semantics 3: Speech Acts.* New York: Academic Press, 59–82.
1976 "The classification of illocutionary acts". *Language in Society* 5.1–24.
Sinclair, J. McH. and Malcolm Coulthard
1975 *Towards an Analysis of Discourse: The English Used by Teachers and Pupils.* London: Oxford University Press.
Street, Brian
1984 *Literacy in Theory and Practice.* Cambridge: Cambridge University Press.
Stubbs, Michael
1983 *Discourse Analysis.* Chicago: University of Chicago Press.
Tannen, Deborah
1982 "The oral/literate continuum in discourse". In Deborah Tannen (ed.), *Spoken and Written Language: Exploring Orality and Literacy.* Norwood, N. J.: Ablex, 1–16.
1984 *Conversational Style: Analyzing Talk among Friends.* Norwood, N. J.: Ablex.
1985 "Relative focus on involvement in oral and written discourse". In David R. Olson, Nancy Torrance, and Angela Hildyard (eds.), *Literacy, Language and Learning.* Cambridge: Cambridge University Press, 124–47.
Tierney, William G.
1985 *The Web of Leadership.* Ph. D. dissertation, Stanford University, California.
Traugott, Elizabeth Close, and Suzanne Romaine
1985 "Some Questions for the Definition of 'Style' in Socio-Historical Linguistics". *Folia Linguistica Historica* 6:1.7–39.
Underwood, John H.
1984 *Linguistics, Computers and the Language Teacher: A Communicative Approach.* Rowley, Mass.: Newbury House.

Urban, Greg

1982 "The semiotics of two speech styles in shokleng". In Richard Bauman and Joel Sherzer (eds.), *Case Studies in the Ethnography of Speaking*. Austin: Southwest Educational Development Laboratory, 14–67.

Van Pelt, William

1985 "Microcomputers and writing instruction: Research, results, and implications". Paper presented at the Seventh International Conference on Computers and the Humanities. Provo, Utah.

Ventola, Eija

1983 "Contrasting schematic structures in service encounters". *Applied Linguistics* 4:8.242–58.

1985 "Foreigner-talk in service encounters: Native registers vs. simplified registers". Ph. D. dissertation, University of Sydney, Australia.

Vockell, Edward L. and Eileen Schwartz

1985 "Using microcomputers to teach college English composition and vocabulary development". Paper presented at the Seventh International Conference on Computers and the Humanities. Provo, Utah.

Vygotsky, Lev S.

1962 *Thought and Language*, trans. Eugenia Haufmann and Gertrude Vakar. Cambridge, Mass.: MIT Press.

Winograd, Terry, and Carlos F. Flores

1986 *Understanding Computers and Cognition*. Norwood, N. J.: Ablex.

Wresch, William (ed.)

1984 *The Computer in Composition Instruction: A Writer's Tool*. Urbana, Ill.: NCTE.

# AUTHOR INDEX

# SUBJECT INDEX

In the PRAGMATICS AND BEYOND NEW SERIES the following titles have been published and will be published during 1991:

1. WALTER, Bettyruth: *The Jury Summation as Speech Genre: An Ethnographic Study of What it Means to Those who Use it.* Amsterdam/Philadelphia, 1988.
2. BARTON, Ellen: *Nonsentential Constituents: A Theory of Grammatical Structure and Pragmatic Interpretation.* Amsterdam/Philadelphia, 1990.
3. OLEKSY, Wieslaw (ed.): *Contrastive Pragmatics.* Amsterdam/Philadelphia, 1989.
4. RAFFLER-ENGEL, Walburga von (ed.): *Doctor-Patient Interaction.* Amsterdam/Philadelphia, 1989.
5. THELIN, Nils B. (ed.): *Verbal Aspect in Discourse.* Amsterdam/Philadelphia, 1990.
6. VERSCHUEREN, Jef (ed.): *Selected Papers from the 1987 International Pragmatics Conference. Vol. I: Pragmatics at Issue. Vol. II: Levels of Linguistic Adaptation. Vol. III: The Pragmatics of Intercultural and International Communication (ed. with Jan Blommaert).* Amsterdam/Philadelphia, 1991.
7. LINDENFELD, Jacqueline: *Speech and Sociability at French Urban Market Places.* Amsterdam/Philadelphia, 1990.
8. YOUNG, Lynne: *Language as Behaviour, Language as Code: A Study of Academic English.* Amsterdam/Philadelphia, 1990.
9. LUKE, Kang-Kwong: *Utterance Particles in Cantonese Conversation.* Amsterdam/Philadelphia, 1990.
10. MURRAY, Denise E.: *Conversation for Action. The computer terminal as medium of communication.* Amsterdam/Philadelphia, 1991.
11. LUONG, Hy V.: *Discursive Practices and Linguistic Meanings. The Vietnamese system of person reference.* Amsterdam/Philadelphia, 1990.
12. ABRAHAM, Werner (ed.): *Discourse Particles. Descriptive and theoretical investigations on the logical, syntactic and pragmatic properties of discourse particles in German.* Amsterdam/Philadelphia, 1991.
13. NUYTS, Jan, A. Machtelt BOLKESTEIN and Co VET (eds): *Layers and Levels of Representation in Language Theory: a functional view.* Amsterdam/Philadelphia, 1990.
14. SCHWARTZ, Ursula: *Young Children's Dyadic Pretend Play.* Amsterdam/Philadelphia, 1991.
15. KOMTER, Martha: *Conflict and Cooperation in Job Interviews.* Amsterdam/Philadelphia, 1991.
16. MANN, William C. and Sandra A. THOMPSON (eds): *Discourse Description: Diverse Linguistic Analyses of a Fund-Raising Text.* Amsterdam/Philadelphia, n.y.p.
17. PIÉRAUT-LE BONNIEC, Gilberte and Marlene DOLITSKY (eds): *Language Bases ... Discourse Bases.* Amsterdam/Philadelphia, 1991.
18. JOHNSTONE, Barbara: *Repetition in Arabic Discourse. Paradigms, syntagms and the ecology of language.* Amsterdam/Philadelphia, 1991.
19. BAKER, Carolyn D. and Allan LUKE (eds): *Towards a Critical Sociology of Reading Pedagogy. Papers of the XII World Congress on Reading.* Amsterdam/Philadelphia, 1991.
20. NUYTS, Jan: *Aspects of a Cognitive-Pragmatic Theory of Language. On cognition, functionalism, and grammar.* Amsterdam/Philadelphia, 1991. n.y.p.

21. SEARLE, John R. et al.: *(On) Searle on Conversation*. Compiled and introduced by Herman Parret and Jef Verschueren. Amsterdam/Philadelphia, 1991. n.y.p.
22. AUER, Peter and Aldo Di LUZIO (eds): *The Contextualization of Language*. Amsterdam/Philadelphia, 1991. n.y.p.